Opening to Miracles

Opening to Miracles

TRUE STORIES

OF

BLESSINGS AND RENEWAL

BETTYCLARE MOFFATT

Wildcat Canyon Press   Berkeley, California   New World Library   San Rafael, California

© 1995 BettyClare Moffatt

Co-published by Wildcat Canyon Press and New World Library

Editorial Office: Wildcat Canyon Press, 2716 Ninth Street, Berkeley, CA 94710
Distribution Office: New World Library, 58 Paul Drive, San Rafael, CA 94903

Cover design: Sharon Smith Design
Interior design and production: Poulson/Gluck Design
Cover illustration: *The Flower Vendor (Girl with Lilies)* by Diego Rivera,
reproduced with the permission of The Norton Simon Museum,
Pasadena, California.

LIBRARY OF CONGRESS CATALOGING-IN-PUBLICATION DATA

Moffatt, BettyClare.
    Opening to Miracles : true stories of blessings and renewal /
        p.   cm.
    ISBN 1-885171-04-8 : $11.95
    1. Miracles — Case studies.   I. Title
BL487.M64   1995   95–3396   CIP
291.2'11 — dc20

Distributed to the trade by Publishers Group West

10 9 8 7 6 5 4 3 2 1

To Julie,
colleague, publisher, and friend,
whose vision for a book about miracles
not only brought this book into being, but created
the opportunity for me to open to miracles daily.
You are a blessing in my life.
With joy I thank you.

I BELIEVE THAT OUR LIVES ARE A KALEIDOSCOPE, not a fixed line from birth to death. And a miracle or two or three or more can occur when you hold the kaleidoscope of your life up to the light and let all the patterns fall into place, watching as each color, each variegated shape, turns into a coherent, beautiful, exquisite, original, and unique design. Each and every one of your experiences has contributed to the overall pattern of wisdom, clarity, and love you bring to your life. Nothing is ever wasted. Each moment of suffering, each joy, each lesson, everyone and everything you have experienced, all contribute their wealth of energetic life experience to you. It takes great courage to see your life as a kaleidoscope. Just as it takes courage to recognize the daily miracles in your life.

Contents

INTRODUCTION

There are only two ways that you can live. One is as if nothing is a miracle.
The other is as if everything is a miracle. I believe in the latter.

—ALBERT EINSTEIN

"It's a miracle!" we exclaim when someone we know wins the lottery, recovers from an illness, reclaims his or her life after an addiction, starts over, falls in love, finds a long-lost relative, wins the race or earns the trophy or the degree or the promotion or _____. You fill in the blank.

"It's a miracle!" we exclaim to our friends when they tell us how the truck missed them by inches, how they dug themselves out of the snowdrift just in time, how they swam to shore, how the earthquake or the tornado or the hurricane or the flood left their home standing. Stories of rescue. Stories of heroism. Stories of triumph in the face of tragedy.

"But how?" we ask. "How did it happen?"

And our next question, if only to ourselves, is inevitably, "How can something as miraculous as this happen to me?"

How do we go about searching for miracles, preparing ourselves for miracles, and even recognizing miracles when they occur? And how do they occur? How can we not only find miracles, but experience them in our lives? What leads us to believe in miracles, indeed to trust in miracles?

The answers to these questions can be found in the stories in this book. There are tales that are testimonies to the power of love, the kindness of strangers, the blessing that came out of the clear blue sky. There are stories that convey the extraordinary that can be found within the ordinary, personal experiences that speak of blessings that occurred unexpectedly, sometimes after great travail and tribulation, doors that opened, otherwise unexplained pathways to change, confirmations of worth, special gifts from on high. There are miracles of laughter as well as miracles of great difficulty. There are miracles of the past, miracles of the present, miracles of the future. There are miracles of birth and love and death and everything in between.

As you read about the trials, tribulations, and victorious awakenings that make each story a special validation of the endurance of the human spirit, you'll soon come to appreciate that miracles not only do exist, but that they exist prolifically and abundantly when we open to their possibility in every area of our lives.

But because these encounters with spirit, if you will, are so elusive, so beyond our logical, mundane, everyday control, we cannot will them into happening. And sometimes we don't even recognize a miracle when it falls into our world. Sometimes we entertain not only angels unaware, but miracles unaware.

This book will help you to recognize and accept miracles in your life. Whatever your spiritual beliefs (or lack of them), whatever your previous experiences, whatever the storms and valleys in your life, this book will lead the way to a new understanding about the presence of miracles in your life.

Out of your experiences with miracles, however tiny or awe-inspiring they may be, you can, as one friend of mine puts it, "come to the next step in miracles." She calls this step "passing it on." That's when the overflowing and abundant miracles in your own life let you become a miracle in someone else's life.

To allow a space for miracles to come into your life, begin by contemplating the very idea of miracles. Right where you are. Right now. Gently allow your mind and heart to transcend your everyday reality, and imagine what your world would be like in the presence of miracles.

So start where you are. And where will you end up? That's up to you. After opening yourself to the possibilities of miracles in your life for thirty days, you tell me how many miracles you recognize. After welcoming miracles into your life for a year, there will be no limit to the abundance of miracles in your life.

A familiar old saying tells us, "Anything is possible." Here's another: "Everything is possible." Here's the best one of all: "And nothing is impossible to you."

May this offering bring a year of miracles into your life!

Ten Truths for Opening to Miracles

1
Opening to miracles allows your heart to open and your perceptions
to change so that blessings can come into your life.

2
Opening to miracles includes using meditation and prayer to clear
and strengthen your ability to give and to receive.

3
Opening to miracles helps you make wise and responsible
and loving choices in your life.

4
Opening to miracles changes your energy level
and your energy field (the field of possibilities around you)
so that your highest dreams can come true.

5
Opening to miracles helps you become a miracle
and a blessing to others. As you experience miracles
in your own life, you can pass on the good to others.

6

Opening to miracles assists you in clearing everything out of your life that is working against you and helps you remain centered on your purpose and your vision.

7

Opening to miracles allows space for loving relationships, and/or changes in existing relationships and situations to support your highest good.

8

Opening to miracles heals the broken places within you and helps you to become whole.

9

Opening to miracles introduces you to your soul and unites you with your soul's higher purpose for life.

10

Opening to miracles leads you to wholeness, joy, and completion, and a sense of loving guidance from your spirit (that which you experience as holy or divine, that which you call God).

CHAPTER ONE

OPENING TO MIRACLES

The miracle is not to fly in the air,
or to walk on water, but to live joyfully.

—ANONYMOUS

*The great lesson from the true mystics...is that the sacred
is in the ordinary, that it is to be found in one's daily life, in one's
neighbors, friends, and family, in one's backyard....*

—ABRAHAM H. MASLOW

On a day like any other, I went looking for miracles. Armed with a tape recorder, pen, notebook, and boundless optimism that had nothing to do with the dire predictions of doom and calamity on the six o'clock news, I went looking for stories of ordinary, everyday people who had experienced or were experiencing or hoped to know or knew of someone who had experienced a miracle.

At first I thought that in defining the miracles I would be forced to trample on a number of individual religious belief systems; that I would hear only of past saints and mystics, revered in history books and liturgy.

I thought that I would have to explain in numbing detail that I was looking not only for the mysterious, the magical, the awe-inspiring, and the ineffable, but that I was also looking for everyday, unexplained instances of grace. The miracles of possibility, of blessings, of abundance, of opportunities, of synchronicity. The miracles of kindness and individual illumination.

I found all that I looked for and more. Both the angelic moment and the humble instance. I found grace and joy in the midst of changes and choices.

Along the way, I found my own life taking on miraculous properties. While I could not walk on water, I could and did find ways of easing and relinquishing old fears, guilts, griefs, rages, resentments. Physical ailments cleared up. My financial life became simpler. My creativity soared. My relationships became sweeter and clearer. It was as if someone had swept the path before me and beckoned to me, saying, "Walk forward. This is the way to clarity and contentment." The more I concentrated on finding and writing about the miracles in other people's lives, the more miracles appeared within my own. I began to recognize miracles on a daily basis.

This is no sickly sweet denial of the darker, more difficult issues of life. Nor is it the "whipped cream over worms" syndrome that I once wrote about elsewhere. To the contrary. I interviewed people who found both mystery and adventure in the most crisis-filled moments of their lives. I talked to people who had overcome addictions. I talked to people who had faced bankruptcy, who had lost everything except their determination to turn their lives around. I talked to people who had experienced great losses and great changes in their lives. A midwife talked about the empowerment she found in the midst of the birth process. A caregiver shared several poignant stories of love redeemed in the midst of illness. A father whose son was fighting for his life spoke eloquently of miracles in the midst of great difficulty.

I began to notice that blessings were everywhere. I only had to clear the way and attune my perceptions for miracles to show up in my life and to recognize blessings in the lives of countless others.

A Miracle Creates Change

The difference between a flower and a weed is a judgment.

—ANONYMOUS

The first question I ask of the people I interview is not, "Do you believe in miracles?" but rather, "How would you define a miracle?" Here are some answers.

"A miracle is a gift," said one man. "Just a gift that comes to you when you least expect it."

"A real gift?"

"A gift of answers, usually, but sometimes a material gift as well."

"So a gift is a miracle?"

"The gift is the change. Mostly a miracle feels to me like something has changed, in me, for me, around me. And then I change in some way too. And it's always for the better, although I can't really quantify it. It's because miracles are unexplainable that I find it so hard to talk about them. But when a miracle happens, you know it."

"How do you know it?" I asked.

"Well, it's like throwing a stone in a pond and watching the ripples spread out from the impact. And the water is changed into a different pattern. For a moment, anyway. To me, a miracle is like someone or something threw an object into a pond, and we experience the ripples as if we are the pond. And something changes around us and within us. Does that make any sense?"

It did to me.

One friend of mine put it this way: "If we would each just practice kindness and common sense and hands-on caring throughout each day, we would all be miracles in action."

A man I respect greatly told me this about miracles: "I have come to believe that one of the essential elements of creating miracles in our lives is to remain in the present, the now, this moment, with no thought of the past and with no thought of the future."

Another friend told me, with great feeling, "We can be transmitters from which peace goes and channels through which love flows. Then we are indeed in the flow of miracles."

Another person whom I interviewed was emphatic that a miracle was not something being done to you, but more like a shift in awareness that brought to you a realization of your blessings.

"It's a feeling thing," she said earnestly. "Don't ask me to explain it in so many words. It's a feeling that you are beloved and provided for and cared for. It's like when you put your hands out to touch someone and he feels like you care about him, except that you are the recipient of the caring touch. And then something changes in your life."

Again and again, I heard this. When a miracle happens, whether you can see it or feel it or explain it or articulate it, something changes, something shifts, something is healed and resolved, and you are changed by the miracle. Whether it is a tiny miracle or a life-changing adventure, a miracle creates change.

Making the Choice for Miracles

In the long run, we shape ourselves, as we shape our lives.
And the choices we make are ultimately our own responsibility.

—ELEANOR ROOSEVELT

There is an old joke about the poor man on his deathbed who prayed to God to win the lottery. "I don't want this for myself, God," he intoned earnestly, "but for my family. God, if you are there, please let me win the lottery. It's all I will ever ask of you again." There was nothing but silence from on high. For three days the man alternately implored and pleaded again and again for God to let him win the lottery. The third day he got angry and shouted at God from the depths of his sickbed. "Why won't you help me win the lottery, God?" he asked in a rage. "It's all I have ever asked of you."

A deep and rumbling voice came from on high. "Son," the voice said, "first you have to buy a ticket."

In order for a miracle to occur, first you have to buy a ticket. First you have to make a *choice* for miracles.

Someone once told me that in order for a miracle to occur, there has to be a change in time (as when a remission in a serious illness occurs), a change in space (as when a truck misses us by inches), or a change within. This change within offers clarity and release from outmoded ways of thinking and being in the world and assists us in welcoming new perceptions and new ways

6

of looking at ourselves, at others, and at the world around us. A change in time or a change in space is an instance of grace, an instance of a miracle from on high. But a change in perception, while assisted by prayer and meditation and an integrity of mind, body, and spirit, depends as much upon ourselves as it does upon heavenly intercession. And recognizing the miracles around us, from the tiny to the profound, from the everyday to the magnificent, is a choice that we can make, indeed, we must make, in order to clear the way for miracles both within and without.

So this book is not about winning the lottery. It is about the choices you make that create opportunities for miracles and blessings to appear in your life. It is not about manipulating your mind for a certain job to come your way or manipulating your emotions so that a recalcitrant lover will return. It's not about specific people, accomplishments, or events. It is not about religion, although it is certainly about prayer, meditation, and an awareness of God in your life.

Perhaps your own life has been so challenging that you have turned away from the very thought of miracles. Take heart! Although bad things do happen to good people, it is what we do with the setbacks and the tragedies that come along that determines a well-lived life. Opening to miracles is making a choice to change your life, so that miracles cannot only appear, but can be recognized and appreciated by you.

Opening to miracles means that you search out, change your perceptions, and acknowledge and recognize and enjoy the miracles all around you. Along the way, you will become a miracle and a blessing for others. And you will live in joy and in grace.

This happens so naturally as you tap into the invisible realm. And soon you will grasp the universal concept that "beyond the visible is the invisible," that there is a source of energy that is the true essence of each person, plant, and object in the material world and that miracles come out of that divine energy that is "the invisible beyond the visible world."

I like to believe that this is true. That just as behind a tragic circumstance lies a story of love and hope and renewal, so behind each person's search for meaning lies a story of courage, of kindness, of overcoming, of renewal, of faith, of trust. That behind each person's daily work in the world lies a power that sustains him and gently leads him to the best within him.

I believe that whether we are creating a symphony or passionately engaged in working for world peace, humble instances of grace can come into our lives and make the journey sweeter and less stressful. I do believe that we can learn to recognize and accept miracles and allow them into our lives, whether we call these acts miracles or blessings, coincidences or synchronicity, awe-inspiring events, or simple loving acts of kindness.

As each of us opens to miracles, opens to the "invisible beyond the visible" realms of possibility, opens to the energy and the blessings inherent in miracles, so shall we all be touched by miracles. Tiny miracles. Huge miracles. Everyday miracles. Angelic miracles. And be forever changed for good.

The Miracle of Possibility

If I were absolutely certain about all things, I would spend my life in anxious misery, fearful of losing my way. But since anything and everything is possible, the miraculous is always nearby and wonders shall never, ever cease.

—ROBERT FULGHUM

A wise man once told me that there are three steps to a successful life. One step is to observe, one is to experience, and one is to trust. To trust in God, yourself, other people, and life itself. I believe that miracles require the same three steps: to begin to observe the miracles that exist all around us, to begin to experience the miracles that exist all around us, and, finally, to begin to trust in the wisdom of the universe and in the miracles that continue all around us. This is not an easy task, but it is a rewarding one. It does not happen all at once, but over a lifetime of observing, experiencing, and trusting.

The very first step along the path of observation is to allow and acknowledge the possibility of miracles. The second step is to come to a place within where you believe that miracles do exist and therefore can appear in your life as well as the lives of others. And the third step is to recognize miracles, no matter how small or insignificant they may appear to be. Only then do miracles, once denied and now allowed, begin to tiptoe into your life.

Yet some people are uneasy at the thought of miracles. "Let's just call them kindnesses or blessings or coincidences," they have said.

All right. Call them what you will. It doesn't take a heroic rescue, a remission from terminal illness, or a financial windfall in the midst of a recession to qualify as a miracle. Although such miracles do happen, and I have talked to the people who experienced just such huge, bona fide, without-a-doubt, in-your-face-to-notice-and-rejoice miracles, you can start with everyday miracles, tiny nudges from the universe, shifts in attitude and perception.

One such tiny miracle happened to me just as I was beginning my research.

A Tiny Miracle

The idea behind the tiny flower is that
it really doesn't matter how small you are,
whether in size or numbers. If doesn't matter how much
you know, or how skilled you are. It doesn't matter how much
education or how many credentials you have. What really
matters is how you affect the world around you.

—SERGE KAHILII KING

Perhaps you would not think of wildflowers growing on a bluff above a city landscape as a miracle. But one day, walking my accustomed path on the bluff along an affluent street bordered on one side by great, imposing houses that were raked and pruned and mown and manicured to perfection, I came upon a sign across the street from those grand houses. The sign marked a stretch of bluff that the city park services kept in order, so that the forest undergrowth below the bluff would not encroach upon this pristine neighborhood. Beyond the sign stretched wildland and woodland and a steep precipice that fell away to the rocks below. Straight ahead lay downtown lights and the whole panorama of the city spread out at sunset.

And there was the sign. Not a "Keep off the grass" sign. Not an "All animals must be on leashes" sign. Instead, an official-looking sign proclaimed the legend. "Wildflowers. Do not mow." And there the wildflowers stood, blue-bonnets, dandelions, hollyhocks, sunflowers, nasturtiums, daisies, even tiny, wild, opened, fragrant blossoms of honeysuckle, all of them swaying, unde-terred, all the way to the cliff's edge.

I wondered who had had the grace and the foresight to put up the sign. I wondered if the flowers had planted themselves, been flung by the wind or carried by birds over the years. Or had some sentimental Johnny Appleseed scattered the seeds, hoping for just such a miracle as this, a tiny miracle, that advertised its own beauty, in the midst of stately and imposing civilization, its own ability to nourish the senses and touch the heart?

I went back day after day that spring, sometimes at sunrise, sometimes at sunset. The flowers spread outward in profusion, the weeds among them waving their own bright banners among the multicolored flowers that changed with the seasons and the rains. The sign still stood. "Wildflowers. Do not mow." A gentle reminder. An order obeyed.

One day while I stood still, admiring the wildflowers, an elderly man who walked his dogs along the same route stopped to talk. You must remem-ber that this is a friendly, old-fashioned neighborhood. People smile and wave and exchange good mornings or good evenings as they stroll the sidewalks. This gentlemen and I had nodded to each other daily, but had never stopped along the bluff to speak.

"They're lovely, aren't they?" I said softly. "I wonder how they got there."

The man cleared his throat, hesitated. "My wife," he said, as much to the wildflowers as to me. "She asked the city to put up the sign. Seemed to her such a shame, after years of being active in the garden club, that anyone would cut this beauty down. I think of her every day as I pass by. She'd like to know, if she were here, that the flowers live on."

He took out his handkerchief and mopped his eyes. I understood. "It's a miracle, isn't it," he asked me, "that the flowers live on?"

"Yes," I said. "It's a tiny miracle."

How many tiny miracles are there in your life? Begin to look now for these tiny miracles on a daily basis. Often we believe that the large, over-whelming crises in our lives are all that exist. During such crises it is as if we have tunnel vision. Sometimes we suffer from tunnel emotions as well. All we can see is the problem in front of us. The last thing we recognize are the things that are not problems, those small and fleeting joys of everyday life. Daily miracles, as in a bed of wildflowers on a bluff renewing themselves each year in a riot of color, remind us to live each day of our lives in joy.

CHAPTER TWO

THE MIRACLE OF KINDNESS

My religion is very simple. My religion is kindness.
—THE DALAI LAMA

Flat Tire Rescue

*We can feel God's presence as real
on the dark side of the street as anywhere else.*

—WILLIAM ARTHUR WARD

Sometimes miracles happen unexpectedly, whether we pray for them or not. Sometimes miracles happen to us when we extend ourselves to others, with no thought of ourselves. This is what happened to a friend of mine, a bodywork therapist and spiritual student who had to go into New York City one winter night for a board meeting of the John Milton Society for the Blind, of which she was a member. The meeting broke up later than usual, and the director of the society asked her to take an elderly couple to the nearest subway stop. My friend agreed, as it was late and dark and she was concerned for the couple's safety. When she removed her car from the parking lot, she inadvertently turned south instead of north. This was the opposite of her accustomed route home.

At 110th Street near Broadway, a block from the subway stop, my friend realized that she had a flat tire. She eased over to the curb into a provident parking space under a streetlight. It was wintertime and very dark and cold. My friend and the elderly couple were wondering what to do next when two large men came over and asked if my friend needed help. They looked menacing and were dressed like street people. The elderly couple was frightened and all three of them were unsure what to do.

Suddenly another man appeared from out of the darkness and paused to survey the situation under the streetlight. This was a Puerto Rican man, who introduced himself simply as Jose. He told them, "Don't worry. I'm going to stay with you and make sure you're all right."

While he stood guard over the car and the elderly couple, my friend walked to a nearby pay phone and called the director to tell him that she was going to be late due to the emergency (she was supposed to return to the society after escorting the elderly couple to the subway). He was concerned for her safety and asked what he could do.

"Don't worry," she told him, "I have an angel watching over me."

When my friend returned to the car, Jose was directing the two strangers, and he oversaw the entire operation during the twenty minutes it took them to get the spare tire out of its rusted place under the car and replace the flat. Amazingly enough, the spare was fully inflated, although it had not been used for years.

My friend thanked the three men who had helped her. The first two faded away into the darkness. Then Jose said to her in parting, "You know, God sends his angels when you need them."

"I know," said my friend softly. She told me that she felt no fear or trepidation during the entire incident. "Yet if I had headed north, the flat would have occurred under the Riverside Drive viaduct, a poorly lighted, unsafe place where gangs and homeless people sleep. By doing a favor for the elderly couple, the flat occurred where it was safe. It was meant to be. A simple miracle."

My friend told me that she was in a state of bliss for days. "It was a concrete example of how my angels watch over me," she told me.

We cannot always explain a miracle when it happens. (That's why it's often called a miracle.) While I was unfamiliar with the area she spoke of, she assured me the odds of being mugged or raped on a dark street at night were astronomical in New York City. It was truly a miracle for my friend and for the elderly couple with her.

So miracles *do* occur in the most unexpected places, and with the most ordinary vessels of kindness, in the form of special strangers directing our way.

Saved by a Stranger

If there is any kindness I can show, or any good thing
I can do to any fellow being, let me do it now, and not deter
or neglect it, as I shall not pass this way again.

—WILLIAM PENN

Sometimes people are saved by the kindness of strangers. That's what happened to my dear friend Connie and her son John in the late 1970s. She and her young son and her husband had gone to the Ozarks in Arkansas in late summer. They were vacationing at one of the fishing resorts along the lakes that dotted the stretch of the Ozarks.

It was a beautiful summer afternoon "on the day we almost died," as she described it. Her husband was fishing and her son was floating on the river, wearing his life vest, while she was reading a book with her legs immersed in the cool water of the river — an idyllic scene, which she told me she would always remember. After an hour or two, her husband went back to their cabin to rest. Connie had put her shoes on the bank beside her, and as he left her husband called to her, "Don't forget your shoes."

An hour later a loud horn blew. My friend wondered aloud at the disruption and then went back to reading her book. A few moments later she noticed that she was now sitting in the stream and that the water was swirling furiously around her. Her son John was floating farther down the stream. She called at him to come back, but he replied, "Mom, the waters are carrying me!"

"I noticed that the water was getting deeper, but the seriousness of the situation did not register with me," Connie told me. "Instead, I kept on reading, puzzled by the swirling waters that rose higher and forced me to hold my book up out of the stream. Suddenly I noticed a shoe floating by me. It was my shoe, one of the pair that had been on the riverbank. Well, that seemed odd. That was definitely a tip-off. I grabbed it and put it up on a ledge behind me, along with its mate, and, incredibly, kept on reading. In fact, the overhang of trees waving in the soft breeze was so beautiful that I wanted to sketch the scene. I grew lazy and sleepy just watching the sunlight through the trees and the play of the light on the river. I couldn't believe that anything was wrong, even though a part of my mind puzzled over the shoe. Meanwhile, it was harder and harder for John, who must have been about seven or eight years old at the time, to come back from his meanderings down the river. It was harder for him to move, and the current seemed to be changing. I thought maybe it was raining farther upstream and that the runoff must be flowing downstream.

" 'Mom, that man's hollering at us!' John told me. I looked up for the first time. Farther upstream, a man was standing in water up to his chest and waving his arms frantically at us. I couldn't hear his words, but he seemed agitated. He stood at the place where we had originally crossed to come into the river, a low crossing bar that had been dry when we came over it in the morning. Now it had disappeared. In fact, as I stood up, the water was up to my own chest! And both my shoes, once safely tucked back up upon the higher, dryer ledge, were floating past me in the river!

"I finally figured out that something was drastically wrong. The water was carrying my son farther away from me, and all the ground near us was now covered in rushing, swirling, ominous water. I realized that a group of people on a high bank farther upstream were all shouting and waving their arms at me. In the midst of all of this screaming and hollering, I saw my husband running from the cabin. He hit the water like a crazy man, and both he and the other man fought through the water to reach John and me. The stranger and my husband finally pulled us out of the whirling rush of water just as it went over our heads.

"My husband was furious with fear. 'You could have drowned!' he shouted. 'Didn't you realize that the water was swifter, that it was carrying you downstream?'

"The low water crossing was dry only once a day, we later learned. It had disappeared under water, and the stranger, waving his arms and shouting at us to move as he stood chest deep in water, had almost been swept away. The horn we had heard blew once a day at one o'clock, in order to warn people to get out of the river. It was a signal that the dam was about to be released and that the thousands of gallons of water that poured down and through our site on the river every day were on their way.

"If it had not been for that stranger's kindness, my son and I would have drowned. Because of the vast running current, the stranger had put himself in jeopardy as well. We were so scared after the incident that we shook. It was a miracle, all right, but a scary one. We were saved by a stranger's kindness."

"We were saved by a stranger's kindness." Isn't that one definition of a miracle? That people we have never met, people who owe us nothing, people who we think should care less, instead care more? I remember many instances of kindnesses from strangers. Maybe you do, too. The unexpected college scholarship, the offers of new clothes and old furniture after a fire, the volunteers who come forward after every major weather catastrophe — the list goes on and on. Aren't all of these strangers, as they give of themselves with no thought of recompense, serving as ordinary angels in disguise?

In the town where I grew up, I learned as a child that for every good you receive, you must "pass it on." If you have an extra blanket or an extra coat or an extra bowl of soup, pass it on. If you have willing hands and an even more willing heart, pass it on. We all know that having more to give does not make anyone a better person. But the fact that people who have an abundance give openly confirms the spiritual law of every major religion that good people cannot receive less than their due. There are times I have forgotten this. Haven't you? But then I remember the everyday angels, the ordinary angels, the angels that reside within and guide the goodness outward, so that we are blessed by the kindness of strangers. And then we pass it on.

CHAPTER THREE

THE MIRACLE OF FAMILY LOVE

*Within a holy relationship, one never looks for what one can get,
but only what one can joyfully share. It is here that one learns the truth
that giving and receiving are the same.*

—*CHRISTINE SMITH*

The Gift of Generations

You have had them. (Can you forget?) The ancient beautiful things!

—FANNIE STEARNS DAVIS

I asked my small sparrow of a mother, almost eighty years old, if she could tell me a miracle story. "One or two or as many as you like," I said expansively, sweeping my arms out to encompass her life.

She quoted me a line from her favorite poem, one of many I had been typing for her "keepsake book," now that her penmanship is illegible, worn down by Parkinson's disease and age.

She croons:

> *We shall creep upstairs in the dusk*
> *To look at her, lying asleep*
> *Our little gold bird in her nest*
> *The wonderful bird who flew in*
> *At the window our life flung wide.*

I have known these verses since I lay in the family bassinet, in the middle of the depression, while a young mother and father, filled with boundless optimism, stood over me and told me that I was wanted, that I was cherished, that I was loved.

My mother continues reciting, speaking so softly that I can

> *How should we have chosen her,*
> *Had we seen them all in a row,*
> *The unborn, vague little souls,*
> *All wings and tremulous hands?*
> *How should we have chosen her,*
> *Made like a star to shine,*
> *Made like a bird to fly,*
> *Out of a drop of our blood,*
> *And earth, and fire, and God!*

The name of the poem, long out of print, but known by decades of memory, is *"The Ancient Beautiful Things."*

My mother has given me a miracle. She has given me the gift of knowing that I am loved past all imagining. Past all the years of family tangles, duties, loyalties, resentments, responsibilities.

She reaches out a trembling hand. "You are my little gold bird in the nest," she says so softly I can hardly hear her. "You are my miracle."

And she is mine. An ancient, beautiful woman.

This is the miracle of families. This is the miracle of generations. That we care for each other. That we see the miracle of mother, daughter, father, son, sister, brother. That we come home again to care for and to cherish the ancient and the beautiful in our lives. That we are legacies of love for one another.

The poem ends with an anthem-like question for God.

> *Did you know,*
> *O God, they would be like this,*
> *Your ancient beautiful things?*
> *Are there more? Are there more — out there? —*
> *O God, are there always more?*

I have my answer. There are always more miracles. I see them everywhere. In every beloved, ancient, beautiful face before me.

A Mother Always Knows

Faith is an oasis in the heart that will never be reached
by the caravan of thinking.

—KAHLIL GIBRAN

A very different story awaited me when I interviewed an older Hispanic woman who lives in Texas. She too had miracles to tell of family connections, that energy of love that flows between mother and child.

"I've always known where my children are and what they are doing," she told me. "I know when they're in trouble. I know when they're going to make a mistake. When my middle daughter eloped with a no-good guy when she was sixteen, I knew. In fact, I went into her room and looked into her closet and saw that her pink Sunday dress and her pink shoes were missing, and I said to myself, 'She's eloped.' Several hours later, the boy's family came to tell me that they had heard from their son and that it was true, the two of them were married.

"Well that's just a small example. But there are others. I don't think of them as miracles or coincidences in any way, maybe you could call it just a mother's sensibilities, or maybe you could call them psychic occurrences. But I'm not really psychic about anyone or anything except my children.

"The most amazing instance of this occurred when my husband and I were vacationing in Monterey, Mexico. My only son, Tony, lived in Houston, but traveled to Central and South America on business occasionally. Since we lived six hundred miles apart, I never knew when he was going or when he was coming back. On the last day of our trip in Mexico, my husband wanted to leave early and start back home. We packed the car, but I lingered.

" 'What's the matter?' he asked. 'Let's get going.'

" 'I know Tony is coming here, to Monterey, today,' I told him. 'And I want to see him.'

"Well, he thought I was crazy, but I just knew. I kept on stalling for time. But my husband insisted we leave. I asked him to drive out by the airport, even though it was a little bit out of our way. Grumbling, he complied. We were driving by the airport when I saw a plane coming in, and I knew my son was on that particular plane.

" 'Stop!' I called to my husband. We went into the airport. There, stepping off of the plane, was my son Tony! Boy, was he surprised to see me!

" 'But how did you ever know, Mother?' he kept on asking me.

" 'I just always know where you are,' I told him.

"We had a great visit and then went on our separate ways. But to this day, the family talks about the time I knew Tony was on that plane to Mexico.

"Now, my daughter, the one who eloped in the pink dress so many years ago, is the most down-to-earth person you will ever meet. Practical is her middle name. But she too had a strange occurrence involving her son when he was a teenager."

With this introduction, her daughter told me her story as well. She had been my friend for over twenty years, but had never revealed this story before.

"It was back in the seventies, when my youngest son was a rebellious teenager. I had just remarried, and there were some unresolved tensions in the family. Finally, we arranged for my son to stay with a school friend and his family until the semester was over, since he couldn't seem to get along with his stepfather or me.

"Well, one night I couldn't sleep. I woke up, sat bolt upright, and told my husband, 'Something's wrong. He's run away. And he's in danger!'

"I got up and saw by the clock that it was 1:30 in the morning. I didn't want to call the family he was supposed to be staying with, because it was the middle of the night and besides I knew that my son was not there.

"All these pictures kept going through my mind. 'I know where he is!' I told my husband. 'He's walking along the highway from River Oaks to Denton, where his father lives.' This was a distance of at least twenty miles, maybe more. I could see him walking along in the dark on a busy highway, and I knew he was scared.

" 'Maybe we should go look for him,' I told my husband. But he felt that if we crept along the highway in the dark, stopping every few yards, it would just scare my son even more. He would run off the road and hide in the bushes, as I had instilled upon him as a child not to get into anyone's car. The more I thought about it, the more I saw that this plan wouldn't work. In fact, I could feel my son's fear even as we spoke. I could see him scrambling to hide in the bushes every time a car passed and only coming out to walk more miles along the highway when the coast was clear.

"So I decided to send him a message from my heart and my mind. Now I had never done anything like this before, but then I had never known so clearly that my son was scared and possibly in danger. So all that night I paced the floor and sent messages to my son. I told him not to accept a ride from a stranger, not to let the cars see him, to hide when necessary. I also sent a message to tell him that I was watching over him, and that even though he had to be careful, because I still felt a sense of imminent danger, he would be safe.

"Finally dawn came. At that moment I knew that my son had reached the outskirts of Denton, and that his father, my ex-husband, was coming along the road in his truck for his early morning shift. I just knew that my son and his father had seen each other, and that his father had stopped the truck and taken the boy in. I felt an enormous sense of relief. I began to get ready to go to work myself.

"Just then, the phone rang. It was the family of the boy my son had been staying with, telling me that my son was not in his room and that they didn't know where he was.

" 'I know where he is,' I told them with relief. 'He's with his father. I'm going to call him at work right now.'

"As soon as I hung up the phone, it rang again. It was my son's father, calling to tell me that my son was all right. I demanded to talk to my son.

"He got on the phone, tired and fearful. 'Mama, I was so scared,' he told me. 'But I did what you had told me when I was little. I stayed off the road as much as possible, and when cars slowed down I ran and hid in the bushes. It was so dark and scary out there. I walked all night long. But after awhile I felt safe. I thought maybe you were walking along with me, at least in my head. I kept hearing your voice, Mama. I'm sorry I ran away, Mama. But I had to see my father.'

"Well, I couldn't even reprimand him, because, thank God, he was all right! But it was the eeriest thing. It's the only time something like that has happened to me. But now I know what my mother means when she tells me these stories of always knowing where her children are."

I volunteered some mother-child stories of my own, and we discussed the forces of energy that seem to be especially strong between families. I even suggested the idea that family bonding and a mother's intuition are miracles themselves. My friend did not want to call these occurrences mystical, so we simply called them the connections that flow between family members.

"But I do know this," she said to me in parting. "I kept my son safe that night. He and I both know that. I've never before or since felt anything like that energy."

My friend and her mother do not entertain themselves by playing with Ouija boards, calling upon the spirits, or seeking out other kinds of psychic phenomena. Their lives are solid and pragmatic, firmly grounded in outer reality. And yet. And yet.

"A mother always knows," says my friend again and again. "And that's the force of family love."

I've Got My Brother Back

In the deserts of the heart
Let the healing fountain start.

W. H. AUDEN

Miracle stories come rushing to me almost every time I pick up the telephone, meet with friends, conduct a business meeting, or walk down the street. It seems as though every person on the planet, if he or she searches long enough, can recall a miracle in his or her life or in the life of a loved one. Miracles abound in families, because so much of our emotional and spiritual learning is invested in family relationships. We rejoice in the miracles that have touched the lives of those we care about. And their miracles spill over into our own lives, in an ever-widening circle of blessing.

A friend of mine told me this story.

"I have a brother, one I love very much, one I feel so close to in spirit, bound to in so many ways. But as a young man, he started to experience emotional and physical difficulties. He suffered from severe headaches, paranoia and hallucinations. As he tried to discover what was wrong, he was bounced from doctor to doctor and clinic to clinic. Finally he was diagnosed with a severe mental illness and has lived a tormented life for years.

"My brother has been a lost soul for many years. No one could help him. He was on a number of prescribed medications, but they only seemed to make him worse. He grew more and more depressed. Everyone feared that he would take his own life, and once he even threatened to kill himself to escape from the terrible pain he was in.

"I loved my brother so much. All this just broke my heart. But I didn't know how to help him, or if he could even be reached, although I tried my best. Our relationship eventually ended. I felt like I had lost my brother.

"Needless to say, this loss added depression to my own intense and volatile life. After several years of psychotherapy, which helped a great deal in understanding my own issues and responsibilities, I reached a turning point. Long-term stress, combined with major changes in my professional life, brought me to my knees. I was diagnosed with clinical depression. My doctor prescribed a new anti-depressant on a temporary and trial basis.

"After three days, it was as if the weight of the world had been lifted from my shoulders. It was the most amazing and rewarding feeling to see the world with new eyes and to see it in tranquillity. I went around marveling at how this new sensation of being in the world felt. I felt new.

"Suddenly I remembered my brother. For years, in an effort to control his illness, doctors had prescribed a series of medications that were intended to calm him and slow him down and control his moods. Well, they did more than that. My brother was continually depressed, to the point of not being able to function. He was on a downhill slide into a dark oblivion.

"A flash of inspiration hit me. My brother was fifty times as depressed as I had been, but we were from the same family gene pool. Maybe his condition had been *misdiagnosed*. Maybe he had been receiving the wrong medication all these years, a medication that worsened his condition and his tenuous hold on reality and sent him into a black hole of despair. One day, in a rare moment of connection, I told my brother about my theory. Desperate to regain his life, he found a new doctor and asked him to prescribe the same medication that I was taking. He agreed, as my brother simply could not get any worse.

"Two weeks ago, I received another phone call from my brother. 'All of a sudden, someone opened the blinds,' he said to me. 'I feel as if I have risen from the dead. I feel like now I know how life is supposed to be.'

"My brother then told me that he felt that it was a miracle. That he finally had his life back.

"I think it's a miracle as well. I have my brother back. Where once he was essentially absent to me and my family, now he is alive and vital and functioning. He has gone gotten a job, and is really enjoying himself and his new life."

When we are connected by bonds of family, we can be both a catalyst and a blessing for the ones we love. Within the crucible of family relationships come our greatest opportunities for learning and for healing. And that's another definition of a miracle.

CHAPTER FOUR

THE MIRACLE OF FORGIVENESS

*As you bring to light, heal, and release the deepest currents
of negativity within you, you allow the energy of your soul to move
directly into, and to shape, the experiences and events of physical reality,
and thereby to accomplish unimpeded its tasks upon the earth.*

—*GARY ZUKAV*

The IRS Challenge

If your compassion does not include yourself, it is incomplete.

—THE BUDDHA

A man I greatly respect experienced a series of financial challenges for three years. Like so many small businesspeople all over the country, he was under-financed and overextended, and at a crucial point in his business life he had to close his company, sell everything he had, negotiate with lawyers and creditors, and eventually settle in another part of the country, where family responsibilities and professional challenges awaited him anew.

This was a man whose word was his bond. This was a man who counted integrity among the most important character attributes. Yet even selling his home, his one remaining piece of property, wasn't enough. He was hounded for unpaid business debts for over three years as he struggled to establish himself and uphold his family responsibilities.

Needless to say, he was depressed, angry, and fearful. "The worst part of this whole experience," he told me earnestly, "was that I felt like such a failure. Not so much a business failure or a money failure, although those failures did indeed play a part. But I felt like a character failure most of all. What I had always believed about myself did not hold up in the collapse of my business and the repayment of my debts."

"You could have filed bankruptcy, both business and personal," I reminded him.

"I just couldn't," he told me. "It went against everything I had been taught from my early years in the Great Depression. I just couldn't. So I sold my house and paid off everything I possibly could and left town. But the failure haunted me. I'm sure it was part of some greater lesson, some greater plan I couldn't conceive of at the time, but my faith was shaken as well. I felt deserted by God. And very much alone, in spite of friends and family. I just couldn't seem to shake this failure. It was as if the very core of my character was violated. I became ill for a long time and struggled through that, too. Things went downhill for a long time after that. I lost some old friends and a lot of business acquaintances. New business ventures didn't work. I barely had money to live on. And I couldn't find a job anywhere. No one would hire me.

"Well, the only way up from down was just constant, continual prayer and constant, continual inner work on myself to heal the sense of rage and outrage that I felt that life had dealt me. I had to get past blame — I blamed myself more than anyone or anything else — and then I needed to reorder my priorities and just keep on going, keep on producing from some part within me that still functioned. After awhile things got better, and I didn't go completely under. I was able to start a new business and take care of myself and my family and even, and this is certainly a miracle, buy a small, inexpensive home.

"So I thought to myself, 'Well you did it. You used your own sheer will and determination to get out of that deep, dark hole, and even though you don't trust other people like you used to, even if you still look over your shoulder for old creditors, still you have started over. You've come through. So relax.'

"Then one day disaster struck again. Just when I thought I had cleared up everything in my life and made a fresh start, I got a bill from the IRS for almost $35,000! It was for the amount owed in taxes, plus penalties, for the property I had sold three years previously, in order to pay off the bulk of my business debts. I couldn't understand why I had gotten the bill, since my previous tax accountant had filed my personal and business tax returns as usual, before I left that part of the country. So I thought everything was okay. I had signed my return much earlier in that disastrous year, turned everything over to my accountant, and paid him as usual. The business failure came much later in the same year. And anyway, the business failure should have counteracted any personal taxes I owed.

"I was in such a panic state when I closed my company and left, I guess I was naive. I guess I didn't check up on everything the way I should have. I came to find out that my tax accountant had left town! I couldn't locate him! He had all my files, and believe me I had paid my taxes promptly and properly for all the years I had been in business.

"So now what was I to do? I couldn't even think. I told no one. I was supposed to fly to the state in which I had lived previously and contest the thousands of dollars owed. I had ten days to do so. I hardly knew anyone in the small town I had moved to in the middle of the country. And it was in the middle of tax season. And all my business files were stuffed in a closet. At least I hadn't thrown them away.

"I went for a long walk. I needed to think. Surely the God I had believed in all these years was a loving God, not a punitive one. Surely I had paid my dues, paid my debts, and could now be free from harassment. Surely I wouldn't lose the new life I had created. Surely there was a mistake and I had been too blind to see it. I kept on breathing deeply to still my panic. People depended on me. I couldn't let them down again, not because of some unfinished business from my past. Maybe I needed to forgive God for all I thought He had put me through. Maybe I needed to forgive the economy, the government, former business associates. I thought I had forgiven everyone and everything that had contributed to the demise of my business and my former lifestyle. I had taken responsibility for my actions. I had done the best I could.

" 'It's only money,' I told myself. 'I've still got my health, my friends, my family. I've still got me.'

"But nothing I said to myself seemed to help. For every reassuring phrase I gave myself, a dozen blaming, castigating words would pour out in opposition. I blamed myself for every action taken or not taken concerning my business. I blamed myself for everything either done improperly (in hindsight) or not done at all.

"I walked on. Soon I found myself by the river. I had walked miles and miles. It was a hot day. I was panting with exertion. I was crying too. I flung the tears out of my eyes with an angry hand. I teetered on a landing high above the bank. One misstep — one more misstep — and all my troubles would be over. It would be so easy. I had done my best. My best wasn't good enough. I wasn't good enough. Someone else could be responsible for a change. I had failed and here was one more disaster telling me so.

"I sank to my knees on the high river bank. I leaned over, looking at the rushing torrents of water below. So deep. So cold. So easy.

"And then I fell asleep. In the midst of contemplating suicide, my eyes closed involuntarily, I yawned hugely, fell back onto the grass at the edge of the river bank, and slept for hours. It was the strangest thing! I don't remember what I dreamed, some melange of cops and robbers and chases and prison scenes, just a wild jumble of all my unruly fears, I guess.

"It was sunset when I woke up. I could see the red sun going down behind the trees on the other side of the river. But as I woke up I heard a voice. It was clear as a bell. I swear I heard a voice. And this is what it said to me: 'All you have to do is forgive yourself.' It repeated this two more times. 'All you have to do is forgive yourself. All you have to do is forgive yourself.'

"I can't tell you what an impression those words made. I was struck dumb. I couldn't argue with the voice. It was as if a solution, the only solution to all my troubles, had presented itself. I watched the sun go down behind the trees, as those words echoed in my mind, and I thought to myself that the sun would come up in the morning again and again and the sun would go down behind the trees again and again and that all I had to do was forgive myself for every error, every mistake, every shortcoming, every fear, and that everything would be all right if I could accomplish that one task. And so I did. I gave up everything I thought I was, and everything I thought I had done, and everything I thought I ought to be, and when the sun went down behind the trees, it carried all my expectations and all my condemnation and all my fears into the river with it. I did not drown. But my self-hatred did.

"And then I got up and walked the long miles home. When I got home, I had a message. It was from a new acquaintance, someone I had met only briefly. She was a health professional, in a totally different line of work.

" 'I thought I'd call you,' she began, 'because during the tax season I'm supplementing my income by working for the largest tax preparer in town. I used to be an accountant, you know, and I just wondered if you needed someone to do your taxes.'

"Yes!

"By the time I got through lugging boxes of business files and old tax information over to her, she had begun to negotiate with the tax people in that other state, who still insisted I owed them almost $35,000. With her help, I refiled for that year again.

"In ten days, I received another bill from the IRS. It was computer generated, and all that was on it were the words, 'Tax owed, including penalties, $27.00.' Twenty-seven dollars! Even I had twenty-seven dollars, plus the fee owed to my new accountant and friend. And that was my miracle with the IRS."

"Did they ever bother you again?" I asked.

"Never. And after that day, that day by the river, my business has picked up, I'm solvent again for the first time in years, and my back problems are much better."

"So it really was a miracle?"

"It really was a miracle. And it's a continuing miracle. Because any time I ever get in that angry, panicky, fearful state I lived in for almost three years,

I just take a deep breath and say, 'All you have to do is forgive yourself.' And my day unknots. It isn't as if I've ever done anything crooked or evil. I just made some mistakes. And it seems to me that the IRS bill was the last great echo of those past mistakes. I guess there were several miracles that day. Someone or something kept me from killing myself. Maybe God sent an angel. I never told anyone about the debt, yet a woman I didn't know called out of the blue at precisely the right moment. And now I'm free and clear. And that's a miracle in anybody's books!"

The Presence of Love and Forgiveness

The course of human history is determined not by what happens in the skies, but by what takes place in our hearts.

—SIR ARTHUR KEITH

Forgiveness takes practice. In order to grow we have to give up our hatred. While anger can often be an energetic fuel that moves us forward into change and growth, in and of itself anger works only as a temporary tool. If there is hatred behind the anger, it must burn itself out and eventually be released through prayer. It is a choice we must make, or else we remain stuck forever at a place that feels more like hell every day. If we believe that love, not hate, is the motivating power of the universe, then it is only one more step to believing that if we exchange love for hate within the deepest, hidden, most sacred and profound parts of our beings, then our lives will indeed manifest more love than hate, more forgiveness than resentment, and more miracles than we can now imagine in our present state of belief.

To practice the presence of love in every situation is no sickeningly sweet or passive role. It is a perilous, ongoing struggle. It changes every assumption that you have held dear, every cultural expectation, every role you have ever played. Practicing the presence of love changes your perceptions. And changing your perceptions creates miracles around you.

The practice of the presence of love, as exemplified by forgiveness, forces you to give up your long-held anger, your ongoing resentments, your fears of the future, your guilt about the mistakes you have made in the past. Love and negation cannot coexist. This practice of the presence of love changes the atoms and the cells within your body. It changes the way you look at yourself, others, the world. It strips you of your defenses and of your distrust. The roles you have hidden behind for years, the persona you present to the world, the ego images that pass for truth, all dissolve with the continual practice of the presence of love in your life.

Psychologist and spiritual teacher Gerald Jampolsky, in one of the most moving, loving books I have ever encountered, *Love Is Letting Go of Fear,* suggests that there are, at heart, only two basic emotions in the world. Two motivating, driving factors. Love and fear. We alone make the choice as to which of the two emotions we will pursue. It is an hourly task. It is a lifelong task. We choose peace of mind as our single goal, whatever the conditions in our lives at the present moment. We choose forgiveness as our function. We choose here and now instead of being trapped by the archeological garbage of the past, or by the questionable future, which may very well change before our astonished eyes as we let go of our rigid beliefs about the way it's supposed to be.

One caution exists. It is a huge one. There are many, many positive, well-meaning people in the world who seethe with unexpressed anger and repressed fears and unacknowledged, unhealed resentments. This is a part of the human condition. So no one is suggesting in this book that miracles can or do or will or should or must occur only in the arena of good feelings and pleasant events.

To the contrary. Often it is only when we are forced to our knees by tragedy and pain that we are open enough to even begin to look at the dark, unhealed, forlorn, unloved portions of ourselves. Usually there is pleasantness on top, like makeup skillfully applied and then frozen into a mask, while underneath there are arenas of pain we are not even aware of. Always, underneath the anger and the hatred and the pain, there is hurt. There is unlovedness. There is an inner self that longs to be received and recognized, warts and all.

The task of discovering and uncovering and healing the hurt self within us can take a lifetime. I'm not suggesting that peace and love are merely coverings to be laid upon the sorrow deep within. But as we uncover and discover and love and heal the inner self, bit by bit, layer by layer, there is room and allowance for more genuine authentic peace, forgiveness, ease, and love to flow into the heart of our lives. And then there is more peace, forgiveness, ease, and love available to flow outward to others. And then more miracles can come into our lives. More room exists for them to appear.

So it's not enough to change our thinking, or to change our minds. This is a first and necessary step, but we must change our hearts as well. And the first place to extend forgiveness is to our self. Our whole self. And let the self experience the love we have withheld from it for so long. Forgiveness of the self releases energies that can and will transform our lives, that can and will transform our relationships, and our work in the world, that can and will transform our relationship to our Creator and our relationship to our deepest, most sacred, most profound essence.

Forgiveness through Nurturing the Inner Self

The child in woman is her growing tip, alive throughout her life span....
One of the labors of adulthood is to befriend in ourselves those handicapped
and undeveloped parts of our nature which we have set aside.

—*M. C. RICHARDS*

I once talked to a midwife who spoke with great eloquence about the miracle of birth. While her story about the mystery of creation and the miracle of birth appears later in this book, she also shared with me her own poignant story of birth, rejection, and rebirth. She told me that each time she witnesses labor, she is able to tap into and access her own memories of birth and early childhood and move beyond judgment and abandonment to a sense of her own worth. Here is her story.

"A life without a miracle is like living in stagnation every day. But sometimes it takes negative experiences, even a series of them, in order to recognize the miracles that lie within us. And the most difficult area of my own growth concerns the areas of criticalness and judgment and my own difficulty in learning to forgive my childhood.

"About a year ago, I met a woman who never gave up on me. At that time, I wore a coat of armor to protect me from judgments. This 'Roto Rooter' woman shattered my armor.

"I was in a place of great grief and denial about my own unwanted birth and early childhood conditioning. As I assisted more women in their own birthing processes, I couldn't seem to hold back my own unresolved pain about my birth mother, who didn't want me, and my adopted mother, who is very critical and closed in. Even as I talk about this pain, I realize that I am judging them, and if I walked a bit in their shoes, I would probably have made the same choices. But the pain of all that unresolved emotion just kept on gnawing at me, even as I prayed for spiritual understanding and forgiveness.

"That's when this Roto Rooter woman showed up in my life. A great friend, she is most definitely not my mother, although she is of another generation. You've heard that old saying, 'When the student is ready, the teacher appears'? Well, this woman friend was like that for me. Maybe she was, initially, a stand-in for the mothering I had never received. But as our friendship progressed, she had a mild heart attack and I was able to be there for her in a nurturing way, as she had been there for me."

"What did she do that led you to release your pain?" I asked.

"Well, of course I see now that we were mirrors for each other, as she had a lot of pain herself about her son who had been murdered. But, at the time, I remember just being challenged by her on every thoughtless, negative, rage-filled, resentment-laden sentence I spoke. We were both working on a metabolic clearing and health-building program at the time, and for every clearing on the physical level, we seemed to have a clearing on the emotional level as well.

"It was as if the combination of the midwifery, bringing a child into the world as a miracle of birth, and the healing of the critical parent issues, exemplified by the work I was doing with my friend, just caused all my old judgments to blow up in my face. I had asked for forgiveness, clarity, and healing, and oh, I got all three!

"Assisting in the birth process allowed me to see tiny, innocent souls receive unconditional love and support. I too am a tiny, innocent soul. I am still a tiny, innocent soul inside. Why should I allow the critical parent inside of me to hurt that tiny, innocent soul?"

"So what did you do with the critical parent inside of you?" I questioned.

"I deliberately got in touch with that part of me, the part that had been running a lot of my life for almost thirty years. And then, through prayer and meditation and a deliberate, careful, conscious witnessing of the struggle within me, I was able to access and develop my awareness of another adult inside of me, a loving entity here to help me grow. She was not a real parent, but she was a way for me to work with my critical parent, to bring that critical part of my personality outward so that I could become aware of its power within me, the power that had kept me from miracles, and kept me from love. I began to identify and talk to several inner parts of me, one of which was my critical parent, one of which was my tiny, innocent, vulnerable child, and one of which was, of course, the loving, aware adult within me.

"Essentially, I became the mother of my inner child. That was a revelation and a miracle for me, that I could actually become the loving mother of my innocent child. I now know exactly how I want and deserve to be treated. I will and do treat my inner child that way. Whenever that frightening critical parent comes into the picture, my loving parent says, 'No! Don't treat my child this way!' So I am coming to my own defense. I see what I really want and deserve, and it is a different structure than what I learned from cultural imprints of my adoptive parents. Instead there is a new, true relationship I have developed with my child. There is a profound inner knowing. I continue to tell my child that she is safe. I continue to tell my child that she is loved.

"I believe that the spiritual journey is unlearning all your fears. The little child inside is the one who carries the most fears. I tell my child that it's safe to release those fears. I know that I have a long way to go in forgiving and releasing the critical parent, both outside and inside, and just giving myself more love and attention and nurturing. But I am much kinder to myself now.

"And so I have become a loving mother to my own child. And this experience has carried over into my work and my friendships as well. These inner dialogues have really helped me to be a more conscious person.

"This is in total contrast to the way I was brought up. I was brought up in a very physical world, a very literal world. With the opening up to miracles that I have been experiencing for the last year or so, it's just amazing to me how my own judgments have changed. I've gone beyond judging people by how they look and what they have, the way I was taught. Now I feel like I can sometimes see right into the core of a person, and see who the person really is. I'm living more from the inside out, so I guess that's why I see other people from the inside out."

I thought about this for a minute.

"In the birthing process, I am sure that you see women who are stripped down to their emotional and mental and physical core, where they are totally open. If you can be accepting, loving, kind, and nonjudgmental in that situation, then those experiences translate over into other areas of your life. Right?"

"Sometimes. I'm still working on that concept. I tend to be a strong, independent, powerful personality. Sometimes I have to just sit back and let other women make their choices and not interfere, like when their mate does not support them through their pregnancy. That's none of my business. I can't interfere or judge, just allow and accept and be there for the woman. It's another good lesson for me — allowance, surrender, acceptance of others' choices.

"The midwife I work with has taught me so much about being a quiet, powerful woman and just listening to others. When she speaks, it's profound and respectful. I am learning qualities of being with others in a nonjudgmental way from her. So I guess you could say that everyone in my life is a teacher for me.

"And everything I am learning feels like a miracle to me. Because, for me, there seems to be a nurturing quality to miracles. Not someone coming down and hitting you on the head from the sky, saying in a loud voice, 'Look at this miracle,' but instead the gentle nurturing self-acceptance where the energy comes forth from the inside and the energy itself creates a space where miracles can happen, where love can emerge. And today I feel that every experience I have, everything I learn, opens me up to acknowledging and seeing and expressing more miracles in my life. That starts with healing myself. I do that with forgiveness."

Practicing Forgiveness

*Weigh the true advantages of forgiveness
and resentment to the heart. Then choose.*

—THE BUDDHA

So what exactly is this miracle of forgiveness? Is it just a nice idea whose time has come and come again, or is it a true miracle: something that can be used for measurable change and growth and joy in our lives? Is forgiveness a force or just a pretty word we have been taught from childhood but never really used in measurable, verifiable ways? I believe that transformation can be both practical and powerful. And out of a deep, consistent practice of forgiveness, transformation always comes.

All reality is relative. It is what you think you perceive, it is your decisions about other people, it is your own personal world view, that determine how you approach others, how you love and appreciate others, and ultimately how you live your life.

If you want a miracle in your life, a good place to start is by sitting quietly and reviewing in your mind everyone and everything that needs to be forgiven in your life. Small irritations and large injustices. You can say or write the following: "I forgive others for hurting me. I forgive myself for hurting others. Everyone and everything is forgiven now, and I am free!" This is a classic spiritual practice that only takes minutes a day.

A more formal practice is to take a seven-day period and write down seventy times every morning or every night, "I forgive _____ seventy times seven, and I am free." You can do this to forgive yourself as well as to forgive other people. Many of us find, when we embark on forgiveness, that we need to forgive God as well, for any and all traumas dealt to us in the course of a lifetime.

It does no good for us to tell ourselves that it's all in our head and not real and that we're too nice and good and kind to really have these feelings of hatred and unforgiveness. Welcome to the human condition! As they say in physical conditioning, just do it! Just do the spiritual practice and see what happens. The laborious, kinesthetic practice of putting your intention to forgive on paper in a rhythmic and disciplined way seems to release the energy of forgiveness from within you. It is a concrete, practical way to move embedded energies out of your body and mind.

If you feel stuck in a negative situation, this is a good way to free the energy emotionally. Unless you choose to, you don't have to remain in any fearful, angry, negative, guilty situation. There is always a way out! Always. Or there would be no point in life lessons at all.

The process of transformation is going on inside of you all the time. When you are able, through any and all examples of miracles, to become aware enough to recognize, ask for, and tap into the transformative process — the miracle process! — then the energy around you begins to change. There may still be problems, there may still be tragedies, there may still be sorrow and anger and gut-wrenching choices, but when you work sincerely with the forgiveness exercises, a release from pain is also given to you. Like my midwife friend who learned to mother her own inner child and thus transformed her relationship to her past and the people in her past, freeing herself up for more miracles in her life and in her work, you too can create the space and the energy for miracles to come into your life through your own personal ongoing spiritual work. We transform ourselves as we grow spiritually.

And when the lessons are learned, the people who are no longer right for us disappear, the unsatisfactory situations fade away, we are released into new ways of being and doing. In essence, we are set free. This may occur in small ways at first, but the momentum of transformation, once begun, continues. And our task then is to learn to love and to continue to love, consistently, faithfully, trustingly. And leave the rest to God. Then everything we touch, everything we see, everything we love, everything we are in the process of becoming — everything! — is a miracle.

Forgiveness Times Three

Asking for love is asking for the energy of the soul.
It brings with it a genuine concern for the other. You cannot
prey upon someone whose well-being is in your heart.

—GARY ZUKAV

Nowhere is forgiveness more needed and harder to come by than when you are rejected by someone you love deeply and have promised to love, honor, and cherish until death do you part. A damaged relationship cuts to the very heart of our sense of self. For if our love is not enough, if we have failed in some way (and it feels like we have, in our heart of hearts), if we have failed to meet the needs of our dearest and best love, then how can we love ourselves? And how can we go onward to love another? The loss of a cherished and hopeful love, whether by separation, divorce, or death, requires forgiveness in the deepest part of our being.

A dear friend of mine, a health professional whose wife left him, went through such a dark night of the soul. "Yet even in the midst of my deepest rage and pain, I felt the sense of angels everywhere, watching over me, guiding me through," he told me. "And at the same time, I experienced an outpouring of love from friends and colleagues that I never knew existed. If it had not been for that dual sustenance, I doubt that I would have gotten through. I prayed daily. I asked to see the truth of this situation. I asked for strength, I asked for peace, I asked for grace."

Several months after our interview, he called me. He was jubilant and awestruck at the way that his life was changing before his very eyes. Here is what he told me.

"I never realized, until the angels came to watch over me, that I had so many unresolved issues about forgiveness. Specifically, forgiveness about the women in my life, both past and present, and forgiveness about my part in all the intimate relationships, including marriage, that I had experienced over the years.

"After my young wife left me, my outer solution was to pour myself into my counseling work and to turn to other women in my life for friendship and solace. One of my dearest friends was a patient of mine, a young woman who is dying of leukemia. Although I cared for her deeply, she was involved in a long relationship and just wanted to be friends. Another older woman friend is a spiritual writer who has gone through some very difficult times herself and understood my pain. So it was new to me to have these various women friends that I really care about.

"The day I was supposed to show up in court for my divorce, I went to a local bookstore instead. In fact, I completely blocked the court appearance out of my mind. Selective forgetting! I didn't even know why I had gone to the bookstore, as I ordinarily would have been miles away at the hospital. I stayed there for some time, just wandering around in a miserable funk. Finally I walked out the door, restless and unhappy, wondering what to do next.

I bumped into a young woman coming through the door. It was my ex-wife! We just stood there, staring at each other. She had on the uniform she wears to work, so I knew she was going to her job. I had never known her to come into this bookstore. In fact, she lived and worked about twenty miles away.

"A great peace came over me. I smiled and asked her to join me for a cup of coffee in the attached eating area of the bookstore. She burst into tears. I guided her to a table and we sat down. She told me that she had just come from court and that we were now officially divorced. I couldn't say anything. Then she told me that she had been diagnosed with lupus the day before and had come into the bookstore to find a book that would help her understand her condition.

"We had not spoken for over three months. We talked now, at great length. I held her hand. We reminisced about the good times we had shared. I told her I would be there for her as a friend, if she wanted me to. We even started laughing together, although there were tears between us as well. I didn't want to see her go. I guess she felt the same way. I suggested lunch. We laughed together again as we pooled our resources. It was just enough to go to our favorite restaurant to eat. As I drove to the restaurant, we held hands.

"When we got to the restaurant, I was thunderstruck. There, next to my car in the parking lot, I saw another familiar car. It was my first ex-wife's car! It was a long, earlier marriage that had gone sour and ended in recriminations. She too had left. We had not spoken for years, even though we had grown children.

"I made a decision and went into the restaurant, with my newly divorced wife by my side. I walked up to the table where my first ex-wife was sitting with a friend. I smiled and spoke to her pleasantly. She was as amazed as I was. We talked for awhile. It was easy. All the difficulties between us seemed to melt away. The years of bitterness and resentment were erased.

"Later, after lunch, I drove my newly divorced wife back to her car so that she could go to work. We hugged. I then decided to visit my homebound clients. I went to my dying woman friend's house. She welcomed me with open arms. We were able to speak of our deep friendship and love for one another. I felt like I was walking on air, yet with a deep and profound sense of the mystery of love.

"I couldn't figure out what had happened. I was too close to the emotions engendered by this miraculous day. How amazing that all three of the women I loved had shown up in my path in one blessed day! I called my writer friend to report on my astonishing day.

"She started laughing. 'Can't you see that it's a miracle?' she asked me.

"The light dawned.

" 'It's forgiveness times three. Every woman you have loved in the past twenty years has come into your life today, and you have healed your relationship with each one. I'd say that was pretty powerful!'

"We started laughing. 'You're right! It is a miracle. A forgiveness-times-three miracle!' I couldn't believe it. And then I did. I was able to understand that there was a shared energy of forgiveness between me and the significant women in my life. Although no one consciously spoke of forgiving, the sheer power of our forgiving hearts melted away the years of bitterness, resentment, ugliness. And it all happened within a few hours.

"Since that time, I feel that I have healed some deep part of my personality that couldn't understand, all those years, why I had problems with the women in my life. I feel like I'm working on both a deeper and a higher level in all my relationships, whatever form they take. This experience has changed me. Now all I have to do, when I feel frustrated at whatever is going on in my life, is to remember the forgiveness-times-three miracle."

Miracles are not Band-Aids. While they can and do often come to us out of the clear blue sky, when we surrender our fixed interpretation of what a miracle really is, how it should look, how it should save us, we often find that we are a part of the miracle, and that our energies, whether released in forgiveness or concentrated in loving kindness, clear the way for miracles to flow gently and lovingly into our lives.

You are probably aware of the many sophisticated techniques that people interested in self-improvement and consciousness-raising have studied over the years, in seminar after seminar, book after book. These techniques often have to do with getting what you want from other people, with manipulating other people. With forcing others' thoughts to change. With forcing the world around you to bend to your will. These techniques no longer work in an enlightened age. Instead, we need to move from mind control to heart opening. And beyond, to what I call Soulwork and what you may call the spirit within.

Practicing the presence of forgiveness in our lives helps us to clear out our own baggage about what life *should* be, what life *should* look like, how life *should* support us. We must do the inner work of healing ourselves, we must, as a teacher of mine once told me, "untie the psychic knots inside ourselves and set ourselves free." And the most direct and conscious way to freedom is through forgiveness.

CHAPTER FIVE

THE MIRACLE OF ABUNDANCE

*What is most necessary for man and what is given him in great
abundance, are experiences, especially experiences of the forces within him.
This is his most essential food, his most essential wealth. If man consciously
receives all this abundance, the universe will pour into him what is called
Life in Judaism, Spirit in Christianity, Light in Islam, Power in Taoism.*

—*JACOB NEEDLEMAN*

The Man Who Didn't Need to Win the Lottery

The only successful manifestation is one which brings about a change or growth in consciousness: that is, it has manifested God, or revealed Him more fully, as well as having manifested a form…

— DAVID SPANGLER

In Chapter One, I told you the story of the man on his deathbed who wanted to win the lottery and used it as a parable of the choices that we need to make to open to miracles in every aspect of our lives. But sometimes you meet people who illustrate exactly what you are working on spiritually in your own life. This happened to me.

Once upon a time, a few years back, at a Sunday afternoon spiritual workshop in Mar Vista, California, I met a man who had won the lottery. Yes! To be exact, he had won $25,000 just three weeks before. When he shared this coup with the group, we all crowded around him.

"How? Why?" And although the thought was not expressed aloud, "Why you, and not me? After all, I'm the one who really needs the money."

He told us that he had no answers as to why fortune had smiled on him. He was about forty, dressed casually, and his longtime lady love was with him. He was a professional man, involved in his own successful business that had something to do with graphic arts. I'm fuzzy on the details, but I remember his almost bald pate shining there in the sunlight and his blue eyes sparkling as he laughingly tried his best to answer our questions.

Finally he shrugged his shoulders. "Hey, I don't know why I won. I never play the lottery. It was just a joke between me and some friends. We bought a ticket between us, a quarter apiece, a one-dollar ticket. The $25,000 was my share of the winnings." So there was more? Oh yes. He had split $100,000 with his three friends. After taxes. Oh my.

"Don't get me wrong," he told us. "I'm grateful for the money. It's a real windfall. It'll come in handy. But it's not like I was desperate. It's not like I really needed the money or anything."

Those of us still struggling with money issues (most of the group) reeled back in disbelief. How can anyone win the lottery when he doesn't need the money? After all, don't you have to pray and beg and struggle and maybe get so desperate that God or Lady Luck takes pity on you and throws down thousands of dollars from the sky? Not this gentleman.

Because he didn't have to have it, it came to him. Because he didn't need it, it came to him. Because he wasn't desperate, it came to him. Because he already felt abundant, it came to him. The money was icing on the cake of an already rich and full life.

So I asked him, "Has anything changed in your life as a result of winning the lottery?"

He thought for a moment. "Yes," he said reluctantly. "I guess it has. First, I thought it had to do with trust. I'm certainly trusting more in the goodness and abundance of life coming to me. But it's more than that. I guess that you could call me a self-made man. Oh sure, I guess I project a picture of someone kind of easygoing and laid back, but I've always worked hard for everything I've gotten in life. It was always me doing the work. It's wonderful that I enjoy my work, or I would be struggling, struggling, struggling all the time, like when I first started my business. I don't do that anymore. I just do the work, and usually everything flows together creatively, and I've always wondered about that. The creative flow. The creative miracle. But that's another story.

"I guess what I've learned from this lottery win is that it isn't always me, or just me, who is doing the work and bringing in the money. I guess even money can be part of the creative flow, a gift from the source, if you will. I'm better at pictures than words, but here goes. Just like in my most creative and flowing projects, somehow I got into the flow so much every day in my work that I tapped into the flow of money too. I didn't grasp at it. I was in the right place and it came to me. You could call it a cosmic joke, or you could call it a gift from on high. But what I've learned about all this is that there is something more than me that assists me in creating the flow. And I'm translating that win into some other areas of my life that need a little attention. I'm translating that flow."

We all know just what we'd do with an extra $25,000. But what will we do now, right this minute, if we never win the lottery? Are our lives abundant anyway?

There have been times in my own life when I have started over, again and again and again, and I have supported other people, again and again and again. And I have wished, sometimes wistfully and sometimes angrily and sometimes with more than a tinge of desperation, for more money.

And I have an abundant life. I have health and love and family and friends and an interesting, creative, beloved career. I'm not too shabby in the wisdom department, and joy has a way of tiptoeing into my life when I least expect it (although I am always ready to welcome its visits).

Because I have struggled with money and abundance issues most of my life, through trial and error and talking with lots of other people I have found what works for me in terms of an abundant life. Living an abundant life is very different from living a moneyed life. One does not exclude the other. But they are separate and distinct conditions. And to live this abundant life requires of me, almost always, to remember three steps to continually creating and recreating abundance in my life. These are gratitude, inventory, and knowledge.

Gratitude, Inventory, Knowledge

An attitude of gratitude is a never-ending prayer.

—ANONYMOUS

Gratitude has been the prime motivating factor for me to change my survival issues about money into a calm acceptance of the ups and downs of fortune. Gratitude for and acknowledgment of what I already have.

Instead of counting the stars in the sky, although that's not a bad idea when we want to remind ourselves of the vastness of the universe, I started by taking an inventory of everything in my life. Everything I had experienced, everything I had learned, everything I had earned, everything that had come to me since I attained the age of reason and adulthood. That took a long time. Try this yourself! Surely a week or two of contemplating all you are and all you have is worth the time if it helps you to see the continuous good in your life. I found that I was far richer than I had supposed myself to be. Even the times of scarcity had taught me valuable lessons in self-reliance, in resilience, in courage, in hard work, in practicing change. In trusting that good fortune will come again and that everything always seems to fall into place. A friend of mine calls this "getting the good out of the bad." It's an idea that has served me well.

After the gratitude, after the inventory, after the acknowledgment of everything and everyone good in my life from the past, I started on the present. Forget the future. Who knows what it will hold? Easier said than done, but a valuable concept, nevertheless. "So forget the future," I said to myself and went on from there. (Although I do have to admit that my fortune cookies keep on coming up with the same message: "You have a glorious future." Hmm. Maybe the universe knows far more than I do and is encouraging me.)

I added knowledge to the mix of gratitude and acknowledgment. Knowledge and as much wisdom as I could muster. What could I learn about the past that would help me in the present to flow into a more beautiful future? What could I learn about old childhood patterns of survival that were still getting in the way of my present happiness? What new skills of thinking could help me past this point of lack? Was this just a temporary contraction in my life, or did I need to change direction entirely? Was it a time of more giving for me or a time to be quiet and receive?

I contemplated the personal implications of these questions.

Just as in the practice of meditation we are made aware of the awesome power of contraction and expansion, of breathing in and breathing out, so too there are times of expansion and contraction, over and over again, in our lives. In our financial lives and in our spiritual lives. In our mental lives and in our emotional lives. In world markets and in individual homes.

Seeing the world around me as a vast expansion and contraction, a breathing in and a breathing out, helped me to understand that I was neither a victim nor at fault in the mysterious world of money.

Another self-employed friend summed it up this way. "The very fact that we choose to be self-employed, masters of our own destinies, convinces me again and again that we are healing our fears about money and survival in a most practical day-by-day manner." She was right. How better to face your fears about lack and scarcity than by trusting the universe and your own creative self?

That's when I decided that what I was, what I *really* was, was abundant, beyond my wildest dreams, whether my bank account reflected that abundance or not. Because I had made a *choice* to be abundant in my life. I had chosen to follow my dream, to be self-employed in a risky creative field, and to live my life so that it was of value. That was, and is, an abundant life to me. And a trusting one as well.

How about you? What decisions have you made about abundance and about trust? This next story may help you reflect on your capacity to create a life of abundance and joy.

Self-Reflection and Abundance

Self-reflection is a gazing at one's life and circumstances as though it were a painting to be examined, felt, appreciated. In self-reflection the third or inner eye is opened, and one gazes at one's life to learn, appraise, decide.

—*Wilson Van Susen*

I asked other writer friends of mne how they managed to turn out books year after year with (sometimes) little recompense. But then, every once in awhile, a blockbuster best-seller would come along when least expected, or at the very least a fee-paid creative assignment, or two or three, to help my friends trudge the road despite the mysterious and unpredictable vagaries of the publishing business.

Here is what one writer friend told me. "Remember when I called you, late at night and on more than one weekend, a year or two ago?"

I remembered well. Her mother was dying of Alzheimer's in a nursing home. Her mother's seizures were violent and uncontrollable, and she kept on attempting to kill herself in the dwindling number of lucid moments she had. My friend had moved from her writer's cabin on a mountain down into her mother's trailer on the desert flats, in order to be closer to her mother and save money by taking over the upkeep of her mother's property. Her sister and she had never been close, and her sister was suffering from multiple sclerosis and couldn't handle the stress of her mother's illness. Their father had died of a stroke after years of taking care of their mother, so the sisters were dealing with double grief. My friend felt hysterical, isolated, and burdened. She couldn't write. She could barely function. Her poverty increased while her responsibilities escalated. Finally, after several years of torment, her mother was released to a merciful and peaceful death.

My friend was released too. "During that time, I called on all my inner resources," she told me. "And I also went though every issue of my childhood, every attitude I held about who I was in relationship to my mother, my father, and my sister. As my mother's condition worsened, I dealt with all that she had taught me and how these teachings either helped or hindered me in my life. Some of the beliefs I learned early on were obviously distorted and detrimental. Those I could jettison fairly easily, since my mother's illness had brought into sharp focus for me who I was as her daughter and who I was as an individual woman without her.

"After a lot of the emotional turmoil had been worked through and the anticipatory grief had run its course, I began to address specific limiting ideas I had carried around within me all the years of my life — ideas like, 'There's never enough money to go around,' 'You can't get ahead no matter what,' and 'You'll never amount to anything no matter how hard you try.' I had thought that I was free, creative, a rebel, a nonconformist, as much unlike my traditional mother and sister as anyone could externally be. But my mother had taught me well. I had internalized a number of limiting beliefs about myself, especially about my worth, and specifically about money, that now caused me to question with every part of my being the messages about poverty I had been given and had kept within, unknowingly, even as I fought to escape from my early childhood conditioning.

"This is not to blame my parents in any way. Nor to blame society, culture, race, gender, or the economy. This was an internal task I had set myself: once and for all to release the ideas about poverty that had haunted me and shaped me for so many years. You would hardly think that something so sad and traumatic as my mother's illness and death could have brought me to such a place of questioning and ultimate renewal and change, but miraculously it was so. Of course, death brings us face to face with deep questions about life and death and God and survival.

"Yet I never expected my mother's increasing mental confusion would force me to examine my own clarity, or lack of it. I examined every belief and attitude and choice I had made over the last fifty-odd years. It was amazing and deeply revelatory to me. And it was about as far from the trite and condescending 'think yourself rich' manuals as night is to day. And when it was all over, when my mother had gone onward into a more peaceful place, it was as if by paying attention to every emotion, by reviewing my life even as she lost hers, I was changed. Changed and freed in some mystical, alchemical way to go forward as my own person, without the saddlebags of inherited ideas to slow me down.

"And then everything started changing for me. First, I went through the rest of my grief, as well as the practicalities of my mother's quite pitiful estate. In fact, the nursing home put a lien against her falling-down, unrepaired trailer, and there really wasn't much else to handle in probate. She died loved, but in great poverty.

"But the strangest thing happened. As soon as I had moved out of my mother's trailer, my own finances started to improve. As soon as my energy changed from hoping and wishing desperately for a miracle for my mother, as well as in my own life of bare survival, things got better. Some kind of energy was completed and some kind of new energy was released. And I stopped worrying about my future. I relinquished old patterns of poverty. I shrugged them off.

" 'Well, I'll just keep on writing and see what happens,' I thought to myself. 'Things have gotten as bad as they could, and I have lived through this. So things will never be as bad again. Things will only get better.'

"And they did. I stopped worrying about how I was going to support myself, and if I was going to support myself. I stopped worrying about my old age and the possibility that I would end up like my mother. I wrote articles, I started teaching classes at the community college, I sent off proposals to publishers and agents, I did editing work for a writer's school. All of these things I had done before, at a bare subsistence level. But now I had more work and assignments than I could comfortably handle. I even got a chance for my first real vacation in years, one that combined a teaching workshop with visiting friends.

"Then, one day, I realized that I was solvent. Not rich, not rolling in it, but solvent. I realized that I was enjoying my life, instead of fighting my way through my 'bag lady syndrome.' I realized that I could and would and did merely shrug my shoulders about the future and all my old worries about having enough money and assignments to survive. I did have enough. I had more than enough. I was not trying desperately to climb out of poverty anymore. I was not rebelling against fate or the system or fortune or misfortune. I was simply living my life, doing my work, and everything was flowing in my direction.

"I don't think there's any great mystery here. It's like the old Zen saying, 'Before enlightenment, chop wood, carry water. After enlightenment, chop wood, carry water.' You just keep on doing what you've been doing, following your own creative path, but because you have cleared away your fears, the path ahead welcomes you.

"Don't get me wrong! I'm far from an enlightened being. But oh I live so much more easily now. And whatever comes, comes. I know that I can handle it. It's just life. But without so many fears and obstacles in the way. And I feel abundant. Okay and abundant. That's all. It's not a miracle at all. It's just my life."

I thought it was a miracle.

Whenever a person comes up from the depths into new life after great tragedy, it's a miracle to me. And more and more of the stories that I collect have this theme. How people are changed by the challenges in their lives. And how those challenges, once lived through, once mastered, once released, allow room for new growth, new insights, new life!

Yet you certainly do not have to have the experience of a dying parent in order to realize that you can and do and will survive the worst and thus come into the best. Suffering and loss are not prerequisites for abundance. Joy, ease, and a kind of creative insouciance can serve you well on your way to a wealthy inner and outer life. Yet my friend needed to go to the very bottom, face her fears and sorrow, and learn her way back upward to joy without the old baggage of limiting and scary beliefs about scarcity that she had been inoculated with as a child.

Most of us still carry some of those beliefs around with us. About money. About security. About safety. About our own capacities.

The more people I talk with about miracles in any and every area of life, the more I come to realize that getting the limitations out of the way is a crucial step to allowing room for miracles to flow into your life. It isn't that you first have to get good enough or clever enough or so determined that the universe responds to you out of sheer will and need.

No, it's the opposite. It's a letting go, not a holding on. It's an allowing, instead of will power. It's the opposite of everything we were taught when we were growing up about how to get ahead. Forget the conventional wisdom. Because abundance is not about climbing the corporate ladder rung by rung, or saving your pennies until you die, or trampling competitors, or marrying up, or getting an advanced degree, or waiting for a rich uncle to die. It's not about any of that. The old saying "Living well is the best revenge" doesn't work. Change it to "Living joyfully is the best reward" and you have a better clue how abundance, deep and high and wide and all-encompassing, can fill your heart until you are overflowing in your work, in your relationships, in your spiritual and community life.

My friend had to learn to change her ideas about abundance in a very personal and difficult and dramatic way. But she did change. And that's one of the clues about miracles. They require change, and they are change. We can never stay the same for a moment, not in thought, word, or deed, and expect miracles to come dancing into our lives. Miracles require a change in time, a change in space, or a change in ourselves. And they come when we have moved past desperation into a calm knowingness. Like the fellow who won the lottery because he didn't need it, we can come to a place of calm acceptance of who we are and what we have to give in the world. And then the miracles occur, because our perceptions have changed. And we have changed as well.

Right Livelihood
(or the Spirit of the Trees)

*If we lived a life that valued and protected trees, it would be a life
that also valued and protected us and gave us great joy.*

—WANGARI MAATHAI

"And then I changed my major from law at Yale to studying to be a landscape architect at Cornell," a young man told me.

We were at a dinner party in New York, and we had spent the last hour talking about his miracle.

"My parents, who are quite wealthy and quite conservative, couldn't understand it. They had programmed me since birth to be a lawyer. I was actually about to start at Yale in the fall. But I knew I couldn't do it. I just couldn't! While I was waiting for the fall semester to start, I took a summer course at Cornell. I wasn't even supposed to be there. But it changed my life."

"What led you to this life-changing path?" I asked him.

"Well, it was really a miracle," he told me. "My first and best teacher was a gardener on my parent's estate. He used to take my hands and put them on the trunk of this huge, ancient tree, and he would say, 'Can you feel the spirit of the tree? What is the tree telling you?'

"So I learned to feel the spirit of the tree. And — please don't think I'm crazy, but —" he leaned over and whispered, "this tree would communicate with me, not in words, trees don't use words, but in its treeness. I could feel its spirit. And I would go to the tree and sit beneath its branches and think. Well I was really troubled as a kid, but the tree would just be there for me. And I discovered that the more I listened to the tree, its true spirit, the more I would be comforted. And the more I would learn. So then I decided that I would listen to the other plants and flowers, and they sort of responded to my hands and my good intentions and started blooming like crazy. I would sort of know when a bed of flowers needed to be thinned or transplanted or just let alone. But somehow as I grew up I forgot about all of that. I put it aside. After all, it was just an old gardener and his magical tales for a young boy.

"But something made me take that summer course at Cornell. Some kind of longing, some kind of whisper, some kind of guidance. And then when I got to Cornell, my first teacher there took all of us out into the countryside, and he had us put our hands on the trees, and he said, 'Listen.' This is just what he said. He said, 'Listen to the spirit of the tree. The tree will tell you what it needs.' I can't really tell you how powerful that was for me. If was just like an echo of everything I had already learned.

"At that moment I knew that I couldn't spend my days in a suit and tie and always locked inside and arguing with words. Words are not my passion. It was as if the tree spirit spoke to me and said that I was in the right place now. That some sort of communion existed between my self and the spirit of the tree. Not just that tree. Lots of trees. And I knew I had come home. Something just clicked inside of me.

"I went home and told my parents that I was going to work with trees instead of arguing cases in a courtroom. Well, it was really another miracle, because after some initial shock and disbelief and arguing they finally agreed.

"And so now I've graduated from Cornell. And I have a wonderful, wonderful business! This is what I do. When I approach a homeowner who has sent for me to do his landscaping, I kind of size up the situation outside first. I see if the plants are neglected or flourishing. I see if they are bountiful or sort of drooping. Now I can fix all that, once I get started. But most of all, after I've talked to the homeowner, I see if the plants are loved or just a nuisance to him. And then I decide if I want to take the job or not, based on the homeowner's or the business owner's attitude. No, it's more than attitude. Lots of people don't have a green thumb, but if they hate their plants, I can't do their yards. It wouldn't do any good. So I refuse to take jobs where the person hiring me dislikes his plants. Because the plants just will not thrive. And I am there to love the plants and nourish them and talk to them and nurture them. But if the owner of the property doesn't care, and I can always tell, no matter how much money they want to spend, I say no to the job.

"I live in a small town in New York State, and everybody from hundreds of miles around comes to me and asks me to do their landscaping. Because they know — and I never tell them, they just know — that the spirit of the plants talks to me, and the spirit of the flowers talks to me, and especially the spirit of the trees talks to me. So I am very, very lucky, because I'm only in my twenties and I already have the most wonderful and purposeful and soul-satisfying life. And it's all because I listened to the spirit of the tree."

Danka's Dream

*I have met brave women who are exploring the outer edge
of human possibility, with no history to guide them, and with a courage
to make themselves vulnerable that I find moving beyond words.*

—GLORIA STEINEM

I met a remarkable young woman recently. Her name is Damiella, but ever since she came to Texas from the Ukraine, everyone calls her Danka. I like to think that the nickname has something to do with the lilting way she says "Thank you" in English. She says it a lot. For Danka has a lot to be thankful for.

Although her story was written up in the local newspapers a few years ago, I first knew her through a friend, who told me to picture a young Russian woman and her mother, sitting on a curb in a subdivision in Texas, on a cold, sunny winter's day, with their suitcases at their side, after traveling halfway around the world. They were simply waiting, in perfect faith, for an American pen pal to come home and give them a place to stay.

According to Danka, a beautiful, determined, and intelligent young woman, the story started in 1989, before the Russian coup that divided the Soviet Republics, in a small town in the Ukraine, where Danka lived with her family, worked, studied English, and went to high school.

One day Danka's mother called her into the room to watch a presentation on the TV. A congressman from Texas, Jim Wright, was holding up a pin with both the Russian and the American flags intertwined. He had come to Russia on a mission of peace and wanted to present the idea of friendship between the two countries.

"This gave me an inspiration," Danka told me, "and so I wrote to this important political man from Texas, and I asked him for addresses of American people I could correspond with. His office sent me twelve addresses, and I wrote to each person, telling each of them of my life, my hopes and dreams, and asking to know their lives in friendship. Of the twelve persons I wrote to, three responded, one from Iowa, one from Wisconsin, and one from Texas.

"The lady from Texas was attending a university there, and she invited myself and my mother to come for a visit. And possibly I could go to school there in Texas as well. So after six months, my mother and I came to the United States.

"And when we had come very far across the country, we found her house, but there was no one home."

And so, in perfect faith and trust, Danka and her mother sat on the curb and waited for someone to come along to help them. Although Danka had learned to read and write English in her high school in the Ukraine, she had never had an opportunity to practice speaking it until she took her dream in her hands and came to America. She continued her story in her lilting, idiosyncratic voice.

"Then a woman who was a real estate agent in the subdivision where we sat by the curb, a woman who was a stranger, came by in her car, and asked us what we were doing there, and we told her, and she took us to her office to get warm and to wait for the American pen pal to come for us.

"And there was such kindness in America, I cannot express it so much, but it is true. So later on our American friend who had invited us came and took us to her home, but we stayed with her only two days, as she found us very foreign to her taste and decided it was not convenient for us to stay, and so I couldn't go to the university with her.

"So the real estate lady, who was named Kathy, rescued us again and took us to her home. She contacted many church people, and then the newspaper came and talked with us, and I showed them the Russian-American pin I wore which I had received from the congressman in Texas when I wrote to him and told him of my wish to come and study in the United States. So then we stayed with different church people, and then a Russian professor from a university asked us to stay with him.

"We also stayed with your friend who had introduced us for this story. She came one day for Russian lessons because she too had a pen pal, a Russian one. But we told her we could only give her only one Russian lesson, as we had to move again.

"So she said to us, 'Don't worry. I will help. How would you like to stay in the little house I have in the backyard of my property? It is yours.'

"We said, 'Thank you very much,' and stayed in that house about two and a half months, until she sold the house. We moved several times that year. It is a long and a complicated story, but that is because there were so many different people who helped us.

"Kathy, the lady who had befriended us on the curb, was the main miracle. She supported us financially and emotionally for six months, while we tried to find a way for me to go to school in Texas and also to work to make money for my mother and myself. But I had no visa for work, and so after six months all we could do was return home to the Ukraine."

But Danka's dream was not dead. She returned to a college in the Ukraine, a commute of many miles from her home. She was determined to get a degree in English Language and Literature and then return to the United States.

While Danka was on a winter break from college, her mother called her into the room in great excitement. There was an interview on TV with two men from Latvia who had worked as camp counselors in the United States, and they were looking for camp counselors to work with them in the United States the next year. Danka applied for the position. They selected twenty-eight people out of over three hundred applicants. Danka was one of the ones chosen. She originally came to work as a lifeguard in New Jersey for a few months. But she was, of course, determined to stay.

"So I came to the United States again. It is a miracle again, is it not?" she asked me.

"But then when I came, I also wrote to one of my previous pen pals, the one from Iowa, and she came to meet me, and I went to her house and stayed for a visit as well.

"The day before I was to return to Russia, the TV had the story of the coup in Russia. It was very dangerous to return at that time. My friend was scared for me. She knew my dream was to go to a university in the United States. So she arranged for an appointment with a private school. I was not eligible for a public university because I was not an American citizen. But the fine private university told me that if I could find sponsors for one-half of the $12,000-a-year tuition they charged they would waive the remaining half. And at that time, I only had fifty dollars to my name.

"So then I went to my friend's church, and I told them my story of coming to America for friendship and study, and they organized a fund-raiser, and so the church sponsored me and raised the money and helped with other expenses for me as well. They supported me through school, and I also did a work-study program. I graduated from a four-year college in two and a half years.

"Well that is not all the miracles for me. In my senior year, I managed to go to Holland, where some friends of mine from the Ukraine met me. We arranged for my mother to visit me in Holland. Then I took her back with me to the United States, as things were very bad for her in Russia. We stayed with a local professor then, and I met my future husband.

"We have been married one year now. And we are in Texas again, in the first same town with all the good friends who helped us along the way.

"Now I am studying for my master's degree in International Law. I wish perhaps to work at the United Nations or in some like capacity. Perhaps I will receive my Ph.D. as well and then teach at the University. Or I would like also to be involved with global trade, perhaps as a translator or negotiator. All this is very possible for me. I am now working for the World Bible Translation

Services as well as completing my master's degree. I am editing the Ukraine translation of the Bible.

"For my schooling I borrowed $20,000, which I will repay from the career I will have when I complete my studies. I also applied for scholarships for my remaining years of study.

"Right now, I do not know just exactly how things will work out for my mother to stay here with me, as she has only the tourist visa, while I now have a permanent green card and can work in my field. But I hold the thought that all will work out as we desire, in perhaps unplanned and unexpected ways.

"I remember that day seven years ago, when I saw the American on TV holding up the pin with the Russian and American flags wrapped together in friendship. This has been a long journey and certainly a miraculous one. Every step of the way I was aided by good people and by my faith in the American dream. And it has all come true! And so I offer you my miracle story. Perhaps it will assist another person to change his life and realize his dream."

We learn about abundance by being in the flow of our own creative path and trusting that abundance will spill over into other areas of our lives. We learn about abundance from unraveling childhood images of poverty and lack and changing our core beliefs to reflect the competent and conscious adults we have become. We learn about abundance from gratitude, inventory, acknowledgment. We learn about abundance from every desire realized, every dream come true. We learn about abundance from giving and receiving. We are then an abundant and sustaining blessing to others.

For the young Russian woman who traveled thousands of miles from her home country to a foreign land, her abundance came not only from challenging limiting beliefs and mustering up enough raw courage to get what she wanted out of life, but in trusting in the unknown and having faith in the kindness of strangers.

CHAPTER SIX

THE MIRACLE OF RENEWAL

The gifts I wish to give you
are my deepest love,
the safety of truth,
the wisdom of the universe
and the reality of God.

—*EMMANUEL (PAT RODEGAST)*

I Always Knew You'd Find Me

Back of tranquillity lies always conquered unhappiness.

—ELEANOR ROOSEVELT

"Let me tell you about my miracle," announced a woman named Catherine. "It only took twenty-seven years. And it changed my life. I call it my miracle of renewal.

"In 1967, when I was twenty, I gave birth to a baby boy. And this act of birth nearly destroyed my life for almost thirty years.

"I was an unmarried mother. Do you remember what it was like, almost thirty years ago, especially in small southern communities like the town in Florida I grew up in? My parents did not support me during this pregnancy. They kept it a secret not only from the neighbors, but from the rest of the family. I couldn't even tell my brothers or sisters. I couldn't tell my best friend. It was a shameful secret to them. This shame washed over me.

"So they told everyone that I was going away on a trip, and they sent me to a home for unwed mothers. There the shame and the brainwashing continued. I was told that the only thing to do was to give up my baby at birth. Anything other than that would be selfish of me. I was told that I could never support my child by myself, that he would be shamed for life. I was told, in effect, that I was an unfit mother before I ever became a mother, and that if I loved my child I would want him to have a far better life than I could ever give him.

" 'Don't even look at the baby!' they told me after I had given birth. 'Don't touch the baby! Don't hold the baby!' Yet my arms and breasts ached for this child, who could never be mine. It ripped apart my heart.

"I had felt wonderful all during the pregnancy, despite the anguish surrounding it. I felt physically beautiful and nurturing, even though I was made to feel shameful about the entire situation. I was healthy and the baby was healthy. But that was not enough. I was not good enough. My love was not good enough. Or so they kept on telling me. The baby was promised to a family who had a future.

"I couldn't go home from the place where I had given birth until my stitches healed. That was because my parents still hadn't told anyone in the family about what had happened to me. I have since learned that what I had was post-traumatic stress disorder.

" 'Never forget,' they kept on telling me, both at the hospital and when I finally went home because I had no place else to go, 'don't tell!'

"No one comforted me. I felt like I was in a nightmare. I grieved for my child that I had given up. I ached for him.

"Soon after I returned home my best friend from school called me and asked to come to my house. I hadn't seen her for months. I decided I had to share this trauma with someone. Before she came, I drank two shots of whiskey to cheer me up and to fortify me for the ordeal ahead. That was the beginning of my drinking career. I continued to drink. Eventually my brothers and sisters were told as well. I was numb by that time. I drank to survive. I drank to ease the pain.

"Eventually I moved away from Florida to the Midwest. I continued drinking, and I started doing drugs. Yet after work I would always stop into a Catholic church nearby and talk to God. I would sit by myself in the calm and beautiful silence and just talk to God. That was the one place I didn't drink. I didn't feel safe anywhere except in that church. I didn't feel safe at work and I didn't feel safe in my home.

"One night, alone as usual and drinking as usual, I got so scared that I drank until I passed out. The next day I wondered to myself, 'What if my son showed up at the door and found me like this?' I tried to stop drinking then. I prayed to find a way.

"In 1982 I moved to California. I worked in an office at a job I hated. I began painting on the side. I could pour my heart out in my painting. It helped. Yet the drinking continued.

"I now believe, looking back, that the universe takes care of you when you can't. I visited a Zen center nearby, searching for the peace and the tranquillity that I never had. Like the church in the Midwest, it offered me some kind of solace, some release from pain. I continued painting while I began meditating at the Zen center. I didn't like what I saw. But how could I change it?

"Then I was in a car accident and I went on disability leave from my job. So I volunteered at the Zen center. I kept on painting as well. My paintings were changing. So was I. After the disability ran out, I lost my job. I immediately moved into the Zen center. I was there for seven months. Seven months of deep and profound change.

"Then I moved out into a little place of my own. Scared, I began to drink again. But after all those months meditating in the Zen center, drinking didn't fit into my life. It just didn't work anymore! So a friend took me to an AA meeting. I haven't had a drink since. I've been sober for ten years. So change after change kept on coming.

"Eventually I went into therapy. But I remember I used to tell the group, 'I don't have anything to work on.' They didn't believe me. Finally one day I broke down in group and told everyone the story of the forced adoption and giving up my child. I cried for hours. I couldn't stop. Everyone gave me lots of love and support. The anguish was washed away by the tears.

"I began going to an adoption support group. I continued painting and meditating. But the days of drinking were over once and for all. Through the adoption support group, I began searching for my son.

"One day I located him. He was twenty-seven, married, and still living in Florida. I had been warned by the support group of all the pitfalls — that the adoptive family often feels threatened and closes ranks, and that the child, now grown, is torn by conflicting loyalties. I knew all this, and yet my search was over. Trembling, I called my son.

" 'I always knew you'd find me,' he said, his voice choking with tears. I told him the whole story. I learned of his life. We talked for almost two hours. I told my son that I wanted to add more love to his life, not take anything away. I told him I didn't want to take him away from his family and all his years of happiness. I just wanted to be a part of his life, now that he was grown. Well, we are still working things out, as his adoptive family and his wife still feel very threatened by me coming on the scene after so many years. But now I know my son. I know my son! And I have faith that we will be able to see one another.

"The incredible part of all this is that as soon as I found my son, it freed up my creative and artistic energy tremendously. I am now soaring with my paintings. I am a full-time, award-winning artist. I teach painting, I exhibit my work, and my paintings hang in private collections all over the world. A huge weight has been lifted from me.

"If you want to know all the factors that changed me from a frightened, shamed, despairing young girl to this mature woman who is renewed by her art, I can list them for you. My stay in the Zen center changed me. Getting sober changed me. Finding my son changed me. Whatever happens in the future, I am changed at depth. And to me this is a miracle. An ongoing miracle. A miracle of renewal."

Consumed by Fire

When we are willing to walk through
of the shadow of death and fear no evil, v
on the other side and experience the (

—PATRICIA SUN

My friend Emily, a magnificent and wise woman, told me this story.

"It was August of 1982, and I was vacationing at Long Beach Island in New Jersey with my sons, Raymond and Greg, who were twelve and fourteen at the time. Eric, the man I expected to marry, and my daughter Karen and her boyfriend had come with us.

"I remember how peaceful it was there. Every evening I'd sit on the porch of our beach house and watch the sun go down behind the large cross on the monastery on the street across from us while the black and orange butterflies swarmed and perched all around. What a surprise it was to find ourselves in the migration path of the monarchs! I felt there was something significant about the brown-robed monks, the setting sun, and the butterflies, but I had no idea what sort of transformation was about to take place in all our lives.

"One Saturday night after we got home, Raymond and Greg decided to camp out in our backyard with another friend. At three o'clock in the morning, I was awakened by a banging on the door. The converted chicken coop

d as a tent was on fire. Raymond was in shock from severe burns, and
as nowhere to be found. Their friend T.R. had managed to drag
ond out of the coop and had rolled him on the ground to extinguish the
hes that engulfed his body. We didn't learn until later that the boys had
allen asleep with a candle still lit, and it had fallen onto Raymond's sleeping
bag.

"I was in severe shock sitting in the waiting room of the burn unit at
Westchester Medical Center. Raymond was in critical condition, with third-
degree burns over 65 percent of his body. Greg was still missing. I didn't know
then that he had wandered into the house, still in shock but not badly hurt.
Somehow he had managed to escape the fire.

"The doctor held out little hope for Raymond's survival. But Raymond
did survive the burns that covered him from the waist up. He began learning
how to feed himself after losing all the fingers on his left hand and the tips of
his fingers on the right one. Week after week, he was wheeled into the oper-
ating room and then back to his bed to recover his strength for the next
surgery.

"I never had a sense of helplessness, because I felt that I was there to
console him and love him. And when he finally came home from the hospital
six months later, I was there to do everything for him: to be his hands, to do
the bandage changes that were excruciating for him, and comfort him after-
ward, and to perform the endless back-scratching that never seemed to relieve
the maddening itch of new skin and healing nerve endings. I had a function.

I was his mother and I was fulfilling that role, but it didn't leave much time for anything else, including my relationship with Eric.

"Raymond had been home for about six months when Eric told me he was leaving. It was like having a wet towel snapped in my face. I couldn't speak. There were so many feelings that I couldn't separate them. Rage and fear were there, and something else very old and familiar — a sense of abandonment that had lurked somewhere inside me all my life. At that moment I felt that God, too, had walked out the door.

"The next two years were very painful ones. Raymond was doing well, but he had a lot of reconstructive surgery ahead, and we were constantly traveling to the Shriners Burn Institute in Boston. Greg had to move in with his father, who could give him the love and support he needed. I spent a lot of time at a support group and being counseled at the Center for Help in Time of Loss, where I had worked with terminal patients and their families before the fire.

"I began to connect my feelings of abandonment to a time back in childhood. My great-grandmother lived with us when I was born. She was an invalid in a wheelchair. My mother took care of her while my great-grandmother, in turn, took care of me. I was the center of her life, and she was the center of mine. I have a vague memory of being about seven or eight years old and sitting in a church at her funeral. When I mentioned this to the man who was counseling me at the center, he pointed out that children can't comprehend when someone is suddenly taken away by death.

"He also said, 'You know, Emily, we're not working in the field of death and dying by accident. We're all trying to heal ourselves.'

"I began to realize then that healing is a process and that I was going to have to honor my process. Two more years went by before I began to feel that maybe I was finally rising from the ashes.

"I went back to caring for terminal patients with a deeper understanding and compassion for the human struggle in all of us. I didn't see my patients as separate from me anymore. I knew that the only difference between me and the dying person was that the time he had was more limited than mine. I knew that deep within we were seeking the same thing — a way to let go and accept. They became my teachers of peace. They taught me that death need not be a fearful experience, but that it could be a peaceful transition into another dimension. They were truly miracles for me.

"I remember one patient in particular. Her name was Lorie.

"Lorie was a beautiful young woman who had worked very hard to make a new life for herself and her two young daughters after her divorce. She was diagnosed with cancer shortly after she had gotten her degree in family counseling. It was the kind of cancer that spreads rapidly. When I came on her case she was struggling intensely with having to let go of her life 'the way it should have been.'

"And I too was struggling with letting go of my life 'the way it should have been.'

"So Lorie would make me sit by her bed so that she could counsel me. We had many long talks about the process of letting go. Before she died, she told me I had given her something no one else could give her.

" 'What, Lorie?' I asked.

"She said, 'You let me do the thing I do best — counseling. You didn't take that away from me.'

"At the moment of Lorie's death I felt her spirit leave her body and a bubble of peace surround me. For two days I was immersed in a peace so complete that the only way I can describe it would be to say it was 'the peace of God which passeth all understanding.' Lorie and I had shared so much pain together, and now she was sharing her peace with me.

"Not long ago I was rereading the book Lorie gave me before she died — *Illusions,* by Richard Bach. As I skimmed through the book, a phrase caught my eye. I read: 'What the caterpillar calls the end of life, the Master calls a butterfly.' Suddenly I was back on the porch of that summer house, watching the monks and the monarchs in the rays of the setting sun.

"My experience with Lorie was the beginning of a complete shift in my perspective about life and death. For the next three years there were many more experiences of walking through the valley of death with other beautiful souls that led me to a deeper questioning of the continuity of life and the illusion of death. I even began to suspect that maybe there was a 'cosmic giggle' on the other side. I have deep love and gratitude today for those beautiful souls who allowed me to share their journey.

"But there is much more to the story. Raymond did not die of his burns. That was a miracle. He rose like a phoenix from the ashes of that fire. So did I. Together we embarked on an intense healing journey that continues to this day.

"Raymond is a musician and composer now. 'The only drummer with nubs for fingers,' he jokes. He has gone to college and now works in musical theater and has his own band. When people meet Raymond, they are awed by him. At first they notice the scars that still shape his face and body after so many operations. But then, after that first moment, they feel a sense of being in the company of a beautiful man. His essence shines through so clearly that people love to be around him.

"As for me, I too have changed my life. Besides my work at The Center for Help in Time of Loss, where I trained nurses and volunteers and facilitated nine different support groups, I was ordained as an Interfaith minister from Columbia University in New York. Now I have a private and group practice in New York State, and I sponsor healing workshops through a foundation I established that brings together individuals from all over the world. Ironically, the foundation I established is called TORCH, for Truth, Oneness, Regeneration, and Collective Healing. How's that for a cosmic giggle?

"Would I have done any of this if Raymond and I hadn't journeyed through the valley of death? Never. I wouldn't have known that such things were possible. Every day in my private practice I see how people can heal and begin again. I am conscious of angels and guides walking with me on this path. As I get out of my own way, and work in humbleness and gratitude, they help me to help others.

"My life has changed and expanded beyond recognition. I am in awe daily as I go about my work. Blessings abound. I am surrounded by miracles. And I am thankful."

"There's another cosmic giggle in all of this. I work with laughter too. Laughter as healer. Laughter as the best medicine.

"But that's a story for another day."

The miracle of renewal is an ongoing one. The woman who found her son is reaching out to build a bridge to a new relationship. For Emily and her son, their shared journey through the valley of the shadow of death transformed both their lives and led each one into a deeper and more joyful reality.

I believe that the miracle of renewal is available to each of us, no matter what individual lessons our lives may bring. Perhaps we are here on earth expressly to learn how to be more loving, how to be more resilient, how to turn tragedy into triumph. Could it be that miracles happen only after we have stretched ourselves, like a flower stretches to the sun after a long, hard, cold winter, into new growth, new courage to live? It could be so.

CHAPTER SEVEN

THE MIRACLE OF LAUGHTER

The need to laugh is as basic as the need for love, security, or faith.

—*VERA ROBINSON*

The Academy of Laughter

The last of the human freedoms is to choose one's attitude
in any given set of circumstances.

—*VICTOR FRANKL*

When I lived in California, I had a friend in his seventies who was as close to the concept of a "laughing Buddha" as anyone I have ever met. He was an old song-and-dance man from the early days of Hollywood musicals and had worked as an assistant with some of the most famous dance choreographers in the forties and fifties. Even though his legs were now crippled with arthritis and he had a heart condition, each day he would shuffle down to Venice Beach from his small subsidized apartment, arrayed in an old red sweater and khaki pants that had seen better days. Once there, he would hold court on his favorite bench, talking to everyone who went by and commenting on the varied, motley parade that passed along that stretch of beach. From the suntanned, flashing rollerbladers and muscle men to the street musicians, from the beachside hawkers to the homeless, he always had a comment or two and a smile. He had a twinkle in his blue eyes, an enormous silver mustache that waved as he talked, and he was a font of wisdom, having read and lived far more extensively than anyone I had ever met.

My friend had only one dream that had never been fulfilled. He wanted to found an Academy of Laughter. He wanted to buy a fleet of mobile units; these would drive from place to place, but instead of people coming in to be tested for their blood pressure or cholesterol, the vans would dispense every kind of comedy. Videos and audiotapes would be available, old movies would be shown, and stand-up classes in laughing would be held. He had the idea that if the vans went to hospitals and old folks' homes (he did not count himself among the old folks), not only despair, but also disease could be ameliorated. He wanted to conduct workshops and include dance and singing along with belly laughs.

Even though this old soul lived in a small apartment and survived on Social Security and the meals his many friends would often buy him just to be in his company, he still thought of himself as someone who had something wonderful to give to others. He brought great joy to everyone around him. I lost touch with him after I left Los Angeles, but I believe that whether he is on this earthly plane or in heaven (surely such a good and benign soul would go to heaven), he is orchestrating great laughter and joy in the sky.

His idea was not new, of course. Most ideas aren't. There is much research in the last twenty years on "laughter as the best medicine." Most health care experts say that humor has a profound connection with the physiological states of the body. Norman Cousins, M.D., calls laughter "internal jogging" that provides a healthful massage for the internal organs. Other professionals attest to the fact that, in laughter, heart rate is increased, respiration is amplified, and there is an increase in oxygen exchange — all similar to the desirable effects of athletic exercise.

Annette Goodheart, Ph.D., a California psychologist, uses laughter in her work with clients. She believes that laughing helps a person take a few steps away from the situation at hand. He or she is then able to look at the subject or problem in question from a different perspective. Something that initially seems so serious can be looked at very differently when a person is able to laugh at the situation.

My elderly laughing Buddha friend had a major heart attack four years ago. When I went to visit him in the convalescent home to which he had been moved after his stint in the hospital, I expected to find a fearful, dying man.

It was a large, clean, well-tended facility in Beverly Hills, and when I contrasted this spacious facility with his dingy subsidized apartment, shared with another elderly man, I realized that by some miraculous sleight of hand, my friend had actually moved up in the world instead of down. I didn't have to ask where his room was located; I could hear the laughter all the way down the hall. His room was crowded with personnel and friends and flowers and books. He waved a bottle of champagne at me as I came in. "Have a seat," he cried. "I'm just telling a few old jokes here to warm everybody up."

One day when I arrived to find my friend's room empty, I grew alarmed. Then I heard gales of laughter coming from the patio. Peeking around a corner, I saw my friend, leaning onto his walker, regaling an entire audience with his stand-up comedy. He even tried to demonstrate a buck-and-wing dance shuffle, and happily someone caught him before he fell.

"Oh well," he said, when he had regained his balance and been helped to a chair. "Enough of stand-up comedy. Time for sit-down comedy. Did I ever tell you about the time…." And he was off and running with his days of Hollywood glory.

Each time I came to visit him, I would find that other people in the facility, both staff and residents, gravitated to his room. It was as if he carried within himself the ability to make every experience in his life an old Hollywood musical, full of laughter, song, dance, and an incurable optimism that life would always turn out all right, no matter what its temporary ups and downs.

I marveled at my friend's capacity to turn a major heart attack, plus debilitating leg problems, into the makings of comedy. But it was more than that, I realized, as I followed the laughter down the hall that day. Even in a nursing home, my friend was still an entertainer. He knew, beyond a shadow of a doubt, that he was here on earth to bring joy to others.

Some would say that the miracle of laughter occurred because my friend laughed himself back to some level of health. Some would say his innate love of life got him through. But the real miracle of laughter, it seems to me, is that my friend created his own laughter within himself, and, mobile or not, shared it with everyone around him. This laughing Buddha did realize his dream. The teacher of laughter got his Academy of Laughter after all.

Searching for the Laughing Jesus

*It isn't for the moment you are struck that
you need courage, but for the long uphill climb
back to sanity and faith and security.*

—ANNE MORROW LINDBERGH

Emily, my "cosmic giggle" friend, the one whose son was burned beyond recognition and then healed, had lots more to tell me about her own experiences at combining her intensely serious spiritual quest with laughter.

Once she and her best friend Debby went on a quest to find a picture of a "laughing Jesus." Her friend, being Jewish, kept asking her why all the Catholic churches always had such dreadful pictures of Jesus suffering. "This was the beginning of the quest," my friend told me. "We were determined to prove that Jesus did laugh. I finally found a picture that came close to a laughing Jesus. When I showed it to my friend, she said doubtfully, 'Well, maybe. But to me it looks more like a picture of Willie Nelson in a robe.' It did make us laugh, though!

"My friendship with Debby began when Raymond was still in the burn unit. She always arrived at the unit with a funny story about something that had happened to her on the way, in the parking lot, or in the hall. As we laughed at her funny incidents the whole atmosphere of the room would change into a lighter, happier mood. She wasn't trying to be funny. It was spontaneous laughter.

"The first time I brought my recuperating son to South Carolina to see my family after he was out of the hospital, my sister rented a house on the beach because she thought the peace and the quiet by the ocean would be healing for all of us. One night Debby, my sister Jan, and I were sitting up late and talking. I was crying a lot. I was telling my sister about the ordeal in the burn unit and how painful it was when the man I had been intending to marry left me when my son was burned. This led my sister to talk about her first marriage, which was something she had never talked about, and how painful it had been for her.

"In the middle of this soul-searching conversation, she said, 'He was in the Marines, stationed in Japan, and I knew the marriage was over, but I just couldn't send him a John Deere.' (Of course, she meant to say a 'Dear John' letter!)

"She didn't realize what she had said until my friend broke in with the comment, 'Well, you could have sent him a Mack truck!'

"The three of us were rolling on the floor with laughter. Each time the laughter subsided, we'd look at each other and start up all over again. I can't even look at a John Deere Tractor advertisement to this day without breaking up. That was probably the greatest moment of healing that took place on the whole vacation.

"When I am working in healing sessions with patients, the miracle of laughter comes into the room in the oddest ways. Occasionally I will see a little angel, a cherubim, flying through the room singing a funny little song that relates to the healing issues of the patient, and I can't help but burst out laughing. Of course the patient wants to know what I'm laughing at, and when I tell him he laughs too because the song always has a deeper meaning for him.

"Debby has always told me that her inner voice speaks to her in a voice that sounds like the comic Jackie Mason. Once at the end of a healing session with me, I heard someone say quite clearly, as if he were standing right beside me: 'So! Now, you should go and live and be happy.'

"I burst out laughing. When I told my friend what I had heard, she said, 'I'm so glad you heard him. I thought I was crazy thinking that Jackie Mason was following me around.'

"As I continued to explore the idea of healing through laughter, the experiences began to show me that laughter isn't something that can be forced. It has to spring from within in spontaneity. But laughter can be practiced. It can be learned.

"A wise writer once wrote about seriousness being a disease. I had never thought of it quite that way. There were so many years of serious growth and learning for me.

"I figure that if you can laugh at yourself, everything will be okay. If you can laugh at yourself, the seriousness disappears, even for a moment.

"I have been told that in Zen monasteries every monk has to laugh. The first thing to do every morning is to laugh, the very first thing. The monk gets out of bed, stands in a posture like a clown, a circus joker, and starts laughing.

He starts laughing at himself. There can't be any better beginning to the day than that!

"I believe that laughing helps you to be lighter and more transparent in the world, whether you are a monk or not! The density just disappears in the midst of your own laughter. It's very humbling to laugh at yourself, especially about your own seriousness. I have read that the highest pinnacle of wisdom always carries foolishness in it. The greatest wise men of the world were also the greatest fools.

"Laugh from your whole body, not just your head. Let laughter go deep into your belly. Let it move you in waves of laughter from your head to your toes. That's the best prescription for too much seriousness.

"So now I prescribe laughter medicine for myself and all my patients because it affects all levels of the person's being. It clears, charges, and balances, it aligns intent, it helps one to go to a deeper level of healing, and it helps one to go to a higher level of healing. And that is the experience of the cosmic giggle!"

Laughing with St. Francis

A miracle is made by using rather than fearing
our moments of disaster. Be hopeful of a miracle.

—PAUL PEARSALL

Emily had one last story to tell me about the healing power of laughter. I guess you know that when you are taking care of someone you love, when someone you love is in a traumatic and life-threatening situation, the last thing you think of doing is laughing. We get so concerned, so embroiled in the drama of the moment, that our emotions veer from sorrow to fear to anger. Laughter is nonexistent. But even in the most threatening times, laughter can be a healing force. And I have come to believe that God sends his helpers and angels with laughter as well as solace, if we can only be aware of the patterns of healing taking place even in the midst of crisis.

According to my friend, "There is a beautiful prayer that I use to center myself before each healing session with each client. It's familiar and beautiful and I'm sure you have heard of it. It's the Prayer of St. Francis."

Lord, make me an instrument of your peace.
Where there is hatred...let me sow love.
Where there is injury...pardon.

Where there is doubt...faith.
Where there is despair...hope.
Where there is darkness...light.
Where there is sadness...joy.

My friend quoted these lines to me as we drove on a sunny summer afternoon along New York State's winding roads, past lakes and campgrounds and forests. I had never had any special response to that prayer, but now I felt something resonate within me with emotion. I could see and hear and feel the impact of the words and their deep significance to my friend. We were on our way to the grounds of a famous monastery of St. Francis, established at the turn of the century. As we walked the beautiful grounds and sent personal prayers skyward at each turn in the path, we came upon a statue of the saint. My friend continued softly with the prayer:

O Divine Master
Grant that I may not so much seek
To be consoled...as to console,
To be understood...as to understand,
To be loved...as to love.
For it is in giving...that we receive.
It is in pardoning...that we are pardoned.
It is in dying...that we are born to eternal life.

And then my friend told me the story of her mother and her sister and St. Francis.

"I had never thought of this prayer as having anything to do with laughter, but when St. Francis revealed himself to me it was rather funny. I was sitting by my mother's bedside in Charleston, South Carolina, in the hospital that she had been rushed to when she had heart failure. I had rushed out of a healing class when I got a call from my sister alerting me that my mother was very ill. I was meditating and asking for guidance about her condition when I saw a figure standing over my mother's hospital bed. Its hands were outstretched in blessing and prayer. I thought to myself, 'This is one of the saints, but I don't know which one it is.'

"Just at that point, the nurse came in to take my mother for a heart catheterization. The figure vanished. I was very upset, knowing that the catheterization was not a simple procedure. I couldn't sit in the empty room waiting for the results, so I told my sister I was going out for a walk. I walked out the hospital door, and there was a huge sign right in front of me that said 'St. Francis Hospital.'

"I threw my hands up in the air and started laughing out loud, saying, 'Of course! Of course! It's St. Francis Hospital. And St. Francis is watching over my mother.' People walking by were staring at me, thinking I was crazy, but I didn't care. I knew my mother was going to be all right. I went flying back upstairs to tell my sister. I don't think she really believed me at that point, but she went along with it and laughed along with me.

"Later that evening when my mother was awake, I was telling her about

St. Francis when I saw something extraordinary. A blue-white light flashed at the foot of her bed! My sister and my mother saw it too. Then we realized that it was St. Francis confirming that he was there! It was both a confirmation and a blessing. The joke was on me, and I loved it. So there we all were, laughing and whooping it up, with tears in our eyes at the same time, feeling a deep gratefulness. It was a miracle to all of us. I will always know, I will always remember, I will always thank St. Francis for being there at my mother's bedside.

"And from that time onward, I have felt close to St. Francis. And I use his beautiful prayer to center myself when I am working with clients in crisis. But I think that it was a great cosmic joke on me as well! And whenever I remember that day, I have to laugh instead of cry."

This is the woman whose son was burned beyond recognition. This is the woman whose fiancé left her because she had to take care of her son. This is the woman who had to leave her job to devote herself to her son's healing. This is a woman who had no visible means of support, who sustained herself through years of operations with prayers and the kindness of friends, and who transformed her life and the lives of those around her. And she is laughing! So laughter is indeed a miracle. And so is she.

CHAPTER EIGHT

THE MIRACLE OF RESCUE

*I believe we are free, within limits, and yet
there is an unseen hand, a guiding angel, that somehow,
like a submerged propeller, drives us on.*

—*RABINDRANATH TAGORE*

Tiger, Tiger, Roaring Bright

*Be not the slave of your own past...plunge
into the sublime seas, dive deep, and swim far, so you shall
come back with self-respect, with new power, with an advanced
experience, that shall explain and overlook the old.*

—RALPH WALDO EMERSON

"I was just a nineteen-year-old, uneducated kid from the wrong side of Boston when my whole life changed. It happened in Vietnam. Now I don't know what your philosophy is on that war, or any war, but I have to tell you, it changed my life. It was December 1967. I was in the Marine Corps, Force Recon (Special Forces Unit). We were five-to-seven-man teams that operated secretly. We went into North Vietnam, Laos, and Cambodia specifically to gather reconnaissance information and bring it back. Some of these were suicide missions. We all knew that.

"It was an all-volunteer unit, and we had all been well trained. I remember the nicknames we had for each other. One of the guys was called the Midnight Skulker, and there was even a famous cartoon about him back in the States. We were all living on the edge. In fact, that was another nickname for a friend of mine, Living On Edge. Can you believe it? I was the Point Man, the one who went in front of the others and searched out the trails and led the way.

I really envied one guy in the unit. He was my great good friend. He had everything — looks, education, class, strength. I knew he would go far whenever we got out of that God-forsaken place.

"Actually, we all felt a lot of pride in being such an elite corps. We were doing a dangerous and necessary job, and morale was pretty high — even though we knew most of us wouldn't come back.

"The mission I remember was this: We were dropped off from a helicopter into what I later learned was North Vietnam. I was the Point Man as usual, and I was leading my buddies cautiously along a main trail in the jungle when we were ambushed. Shots were fired all around us. I heard a lot of yelling and screaming. We started returning fire, but it was too late. My buddies fell. Just crumbled. Just shot down in cold blood. It was so unexpected, and we were completely outnumbered. I was knocked out by a gun butt. When I came to, I found myself tied and gagged. There were eight North Vietnamese guys and me. My team was dead. I was lost in the jungle, trussed like a turkey, outnumbered eight to one, as they dragged me along a trail for days.

"I don't know to this day why they didn't kill me on the spot. They wanted a prisoner, I guess. Maybe they wanted information. That's what I thought when they stopped dragging me along the trail, pushed me upright, and loosened my bound feet a little so that I could stand. My arms were still tied behind my back, but they took my blindfold off. They were looking at a map and gesticulating with waving arms. I thought maybe they were lost. But when they shoved the map in front of me and tried to say 'Show me' in broken English, I figured out that what they wanted from me were U.S. positions. Well, I couldn't tell them, even if I had wanted to, because I didn't know where I was or where the U.S. positions were in relationship to the jungle I had been dragged through for days.

"You've got to remember, I was just a short, skinny young kid — well trained as a Marine, but young and scared and thinking I would die any minute, as soon as my usefulness to my captors was over. I couldn't even process the fact that my buddies had died. Why them and not me? What did I have to offer? I was nobody special. I really thought I would die any minute, even though I hadn't really lived my life yet. So there was some regret along with knowing that I didn't have a chance with eight guys to one in the middle of enemy territory.

"But I didn't want to die. And so I prayed for a miracle and tried to keep my wits about me, even though I was hungry and thirsty and my head was pounding from the wound the gun butt had left along the side of my head. When I couldn't seem to help my captors with the map, one put his AK47 to my forehead. There was another guy behind me with his weapon nudging my back. For some reason, they cut my arms free then, I guess to give me one last chance to show them the positions they wanted on the map.

"Then something happened I will never be able to explain to this day.

"A tiger roared.

"All of them jumped in fear.

"It was as if God had said, 'NOW!' I moved my left arm and knocked aside the weapon pointed at my forehead with one thrust of my arm. I grabbed the weapon from the guy behind me, knocked the two of them over, and started shooting. Then I ran like hell.

"I didn't know where I was going. It was dense jungle and near nightfall. I didn't want to get too far off the main trail because I knew I had to find my way back to the pickup point where the helicopters left us off and picked us up. That is, if anyone thought that any of our mission team was still alive. But the main trail was where the enemy troops came in, too. I had known all along that the best I could hope for from my captors was torture and death. But now I was free! By some miracle, I was free! The weapon I had wrestled from my captors was empty now, just useful as a club if anyone came along. I was praying like hell.

"I prayed for three days and for three nights. Yes, it's true. My life *did* flash before my eyes. 'Why didn't I go to college? Why didn't I marry? Why didn't I make something of myself?'

"I thought of the guy in my unit who seemed to have all the advantages. Why had he been killed and I spared? No food, no water. I had a lot of time to think. I thought that I had really screwed up, even though now, in retrospect, I don't see what else a skinny runt of a nineteen-year-old could have done with his life at that point. But I was alive! That *was* the point.

"Then I heard the copter. I was close to the extraction site. That was another miracle! Because if you're not there when the copter comes, too bad. But they found me. They found me and took me back to base.

"It was the most miraculous thing that had ever happened to me. So I kept on asking God, 'Why did you let me live? My friends died. Why did you let me live? What can I make of my life? You've given me my life. What can I do with it? You tell me, God, and I'll do it.'

"I had joined the Marines as an idealistic kid wanting to save lives. Now my life had been saved. It had to mean something — something important. I remembered how my father always put me down. I remembered how nobody thought I would even get through high school. One time I told somebody at school, a teacher or counselor, that I wanted to go to college. I wanted to go to medical school. I wanted to save lives. I wanted to do something that made a difference in the world. I wanted to make a contribution to life in some way. And that teacher laughed at me. He said I didn't have a chance.

"But I did have a chance. A second chance. Another chance. And I figured that if I could survive the last few days I had gone through, I could do anything. Anything! And I wanted to give back something because my life had been saved. It was a turning point for me. I vowed I would do something with my life after my tour was over. And I did.

"I applied to college. I had the GI Bill. And then I applied to Boston Medical School. And I found mentors along the way. And it's all because a tiger roared! It's all because of that. And of course you know the rest and what I do now."

I did know. My friend is a caring psychotherapist, attached to a local hospital as part of the hospice care. He spends his days and nights helping patients come to acceptance and closure at the end of their lives. He gently encourages the patients' families to come to resolution, express their grief, and then go on after their loved one has died. He assists people to find meaning as the survivors. He helps people to make peace with themselves and go forward.

My friend recognizes miracles all around him. Although he still has challenges in his personal life, he knows that miracles do come to pass and that there is someone who looks out for him and helps him reach the people in his care. And all because a tiger roared in the jungles of North Vietnam and a kid escaped to take back his life.

Lifted Up to Live Again

The great secret is this:
Consider yourself a part of the universe
And a part of the eternal stream of time:
Consider your life to be a true miracle;
And put to God all the questions you may have.

—ROBERT MULLER

A friend told me this story only recently, although I have known her for years. She is a down-to-earth, commonsense, practical woman. I do not doubt her words. This is what she told me.

"I was coming home from the grocery store, with three sacks of groceries on the floor of the backseat of my car. I slowed to a stop to turn left at a light. Another car had come to a stop in front of me and was also waiting to turn. I happened to glance into my rearview mirror. I saw an old gray convertible speeding toward me at what I later learned was in excess of eighty miles an hour. There were cars in the lane next to me, so I couldn't cross over into that lane. And the traffic coming toward me was heavy as well. I knew I was going to be hit. Because of my seat belt, I didn't even have time to move into the passenger seat.

" 'God save me!' I prayed again and again. 'God help me, God save me!'

"It all happened in an instant. The old gray convertible crashed into the rear of my car head-on. My car crashed into the stopped car in front of me. The old convertible spun and crashed into a third car blocking the right-hand lane. Revving its motor, it sped around the wreckage of the three cars and roared on. But I was not in the wreckage. I was sitting on the curb at the side of the road.

"I looked at my car. The force of the collision had crumpled it like an accordion. The groceries had been pushed through the back of the front seat, into the front of the car on the driver's side, where I had been. The steering wheel had been forced through the front of the car and through the shattered windshield. The car was totaled. The car in front of mine was also damaged, as was the car in the right-hand lane that the driver had sideswiped getting away.

"I don't remember anything past the sound of the crash. I didn't feel anything. Instead it was as if time stood still for a moment before the crash. I heard the sound but felt nothing. That's because I was literally lifted up by something, someone, and deposited safely on the curb. I felt as if my body was not quite there, as if my mind and my body didn't quite match up. I thought it was the shock. I did have minor bruises, as if the car had hit me after all. But I was not there! The car was destroyed, but I was sitting on the curb looking at my totaled car.

"Someone in the row of houses along the street called the police and the ambulances. They even called my husband and told him to come get me, that I was okay, not a scratch on me, just dazed and in shock. It turned out later that no one was hurt badly except the driver of the gray convertible. He was on some kind of drugs, and it was a stolen car. There were attempts by the other drivers and by my husband to collect damages, but nothing ever came of it.

"I went home, and it was the weirdest situation: For several days as I walked around the house, I could see my body out in front of me, not part of me, just out in front of me, and I had to remember each time to walk into my body and fit inside of it properly. It looked like a shadow in front of me. I had to walk into the back of it. I had to make my body fit me again. After awhile, this sensation of being out of my body, of observing my body from a distance, went away. Things got back to normal.

"I don't know why I was saved that day from certain death. I guess it wasn't my time. I guess there is more for me to do. But that incident convinced me that God is real. I can still feel that sensation of being lifted up and out of the car and deposited on the curb, and sometimes I can even see my body sitting on the curb as I am being lifted out of the car. I see it sitting there waiting for me to be deposited within its familiar contours. It's an eerie sensation, and one I will never forget. I just know it was a miracle.

"I always believed in God, but it was just an intellectual belief, even though I feel like I am a good person. But now I know. Now I know! I feel like I have been lifted up to live again. I know that God has a plan and a purpose for my life, and that I've got lots more work to do here on earth."

Miracles occur as a change in time, a change in space, or a change in perception. Sometimes all three change. Out of a change in time, a change in space, or a change in perception, we change. We change our attitudes. We change our behavior patterns. We change the way we look at ourselves, the people in our lives, and the world around us. Sometimes we change direction. Sometimes we change our ideas about God. Sometimes we even open to angels, or at least the possibility of angels, watching over us in our lives.

While I was in the process of collecting miracle stories for this book, a friend asked me why so many interviews had to do with the challenges of life. "Aren't there ever any times when miracles just fall out of the clear blue sky when you least expect them? Without all this anguish, without all this wishing and hoping?"

Miracles do not require anguish. And miracles are never about wishing and hoping. If they were, all of us would have a pocketful of miracles to report and to treasure. According to Paul Pearsall in *Making Miracles,* "Wishing denotes a request for intervention from 'without'…. Miracle making represents a discovery of a new way of knowing from 'within'. If wishing is longing for love, then miracle making is active loving through every crisis and challenge in daily living."

Sometimes it is only when we are faced with life-threatening challenges that changes take place. And change is one of the signs of a miracle. Something changes. We get better. We decide to do something different. We change our thoughts and ideas and attitudes and behavior about whatever it is that we are seeking to change in our lives. We shift our perceptions. We see more clearly or more broadly or more deeply. We change. And then and only then can the miracle be allowed into our lives. Whether it tiptoes in like the spirit of trees speaking to us or tosses us up into the air in rescue, miracles change us. We are never the same again. Not for a moment.

And as we shift and change and allow and recognize miracles in our lives, it doesn't matter by what name we call the change — call it coincidence or synchronicity, or call it a blessing, or call it magical or mysterious or otherworldly, or say that we were saved by the bell or caught in the nick of time — still, when miracles come, we are changed forever. And the more they come, the easier it is to recognize miracles in our daily lives, and the more we can live our lives in renewal and gratitude, instead of desperation. Instead of wishing and hoping and praying hard, we can allow and accept and embrace the myriad evidence of miracles all around us, just waiting to be recognized.

Then our lives become an endless steady stream of miracle awareness. And we are blessed. And we are renewed. And we are loved and loving. Yes!

CHAPTER NINE

THE MIRACLE OF ANGELS OF COMFORT AND GENTLE GHOSTS

*Be not afraid to have
strangers in your house,
for some thereby have
entertained angels unawares.*

—*HEBREWS 13:2*

Angels of Comfort and Joy

Faith grows stronger by exercise.

—ANONYMOUS

Here is what a dear friend told me of his experiences with angels of comfort and joy.

"I like to think that our process of becoming spiritually sensitive is much like tuning in to a radio or television broadcast, because our inner universe seems to operate on certain frequencies that lie beyond ordinary, everyday reality. Think of it like this: Wherever you may be at this moment, there are countless numbers of radio waves and different frequencies of sound and light all around you. Yet you are unaware of these because you do not have your receiving unit tuned to an appropriate transmitting frequency. Let's say that some important news message was being transmitted on every radio station in your area. Without your receiver turned on and tuned to a transmitting station, you would not be aware of what was being reported, and you would be oblivious to what was happening in your world.

"Similarly, when we are not spiritually attuned to the messages from our universe, whether they come from our dreams or intuition or from other naggings in our spirit, we cannot possibly be aware of all the information that is available to us for our life's decisions.

"If all that is to be is already known on another level or in another realm, think of the awesome implications. Just imagine: If we could tune into those frequencies, it would then be possible for us to know about certain imminent situations just around the corner in our lives. We could then prepare for them and be more able to accept, resolve, or use these coming events as a learning experience in some way. Maybe, too, we could then see our lives as not being quite so serious in the larger scope of the universe.

"Even as I say these things, I realize that often I have not been tuned into the greater reality of my life's unfolding. Even though I had the sense of angels around me, protecting me and leading me, it is only in retrospect that I can see the pattern unfolding.

"Take my personal situation of the last few months. After being married for only five months, to a much younger woman who had been the daughter of one of my dying patients, I began to have an affinity for angels. Books about angels, figurine likenesses of angels, angels in every shape and form intruded on my vision. Because I work in the cancer ward of a large hospital, helping dying patients and their families, I believed that the angels were there for them, but not for me. But because of my preoccupation with angels, I did grow closer to God and began to feel a sense of safety and love which previously I had only contemplated conceptually. I began to find solace in my most worrisome and painful moments. I truly felt the presence of a profound peace, no matter what seemed to be going on at the moment.

"Then, after a few months of sensing that some ominous event must be looming ahead, ready to swoop down upon me, I came home one evening after a cancer support group to find a bare apartment, with only my bed and clothing still there. My wife had left, without any warning, with no communication about her decision and with no explanation.

"I felt a horrible shock, and then, just as instantly, a loving and profound peace. At that moment, I recalled how only eight years before I had experienced this same presence of peace. It came just before I found my father only minutes after a self-inflicted gunshot wound to his head took his life. The suicide of my father was as unexpected as the loss of my wife. Yet here I stood, enveloped in a profound peace.

"Were both of these events instances where angels had really rescued me and swept me up with their wings in an act of nurturing and love? I believe this to be true.

"As I reflected on both experiences, I realized that I had experienced a kind of foreknowledge that no matter what happened I would feel safe and know that everything was as it was meant to be and that I was going to be okay.

"I'd like to say that what I experienced in both traumatic instances was a miracle. It felt like that to me. It felt like someone or something much greater than I cared about me at these two dark moments of my life.

"This sense of peace helps me to go forward in my work. Maybe angels are there for everyone, and we just have to tap into their reality. Maybe. I hope it's true."

Gentle Ghosts

It is only with the heart that one can see rightly.
What is essential is invisible to the eye.

—ANTOINE DE SAINT-EXUPERY

For another woman, a dear, elderly friend of mine, angels did not appear to her at the end of her life, although she is a devout and traditional churchgoer. Instead, what she called "gentle ghosts" came to help her through months of crisis. Here is her story.

"Being a secretary for many years, I deal in business facts, not fantasy. I'm probably the most practical and down-to-earth person you'll ever meet. The only fantasy movie I ever went to was *E.T.*, and I cried my way all through that one, along with my grandchildren.

"So I never expected a trio of gentle ghosts to establish themselves in my home. In fact, I was thoroughly surprised when they did.

"I had been somewhat despondent for months, going through round after round of lab tests and worrying over the doctors' failure to discover a reason why I was wasting away. But at least I had all my faculties, or so I told myself and my close friends. I tried to joke about my condition and ended more than one conversation with the mock wail of a child: 'I want my mother!'

"My friends laughed, but I often went home thinking about how close I had felt to my beloved mother during all the years she cared for me and all the years I cared for her. Even though we said good-bye at the cemetery, I thought of her every day and quoted all of the little sayings she was so fond of telling me.

"Well, she must have heard me. She must have heard the panic beneath my cry for help, because several weeks later, as I entered my apartment, I knew instantly that my mother was there. I couldn't catch her scent, for she never wore perfume. And I couldn't quite catch sight of her in any of the rooms of my apartment, but I knew she was there. Without a doubt, I knew that my mother was there. There was an aura of a fire that had just been extinguished — that's the best way I can put it. A glow of love. I could feel my mother's love surrounding me, cherishing me. I just knew she was there, so close, so sweet, so near and dear.

"I sat down in the first chair I touched. Then I sank down into the warmth of love surrounding me. I just let myself be in the light and love of her presence. Soon I was conscious of two other presences as well. I did not see any clothing or bodies. No one spoke.

"Soon I gave up wondering about all of this and just allowed myself to feel the presence of my dear mother and the other two gentle ghosts.

"How I wish that I could say that I could really see my dear mother in the flesh or touch her or have her touch me. But that was not to be. Not yet, anyway.

"This was not one of those life-after-death experiences that you read about. There was no steady beam or brilliant light leading onward through a dark tunnel, no feeling of hovering above the surgery table, no knowing for a moment or two that you had indeed died and then seen God.

"But my prayers were answered. I had cried out for my mother, and she came to me. This was a miracle to me. She came to me again and again. I even feel her presence now, as I write these words. This may not be your everyday miracle, but it has put me in the believer's corner for what is left of my life.

"I soon figured out that the other two gentle ghosts that had taken up residence in my home were my younger sister and my only brother.

"I don't really know why God sent my brother and sister to my home to be ghosts as well. I wasn't particularly close to my brother as we grew up, but he didn't have long to be a young man anyway, as his plane crashed in World War II on a training flight just two days after his marriage. He was only eighteen years old. It was a long time ago. But I remember him always as a lean, smiling, mischievous boy with sparkling blue eyes, who teased me sometimes, yet never made me cry. He was always ready to help me do my hard chores. I'm afraid I even took advantage of his good humor. Once in awhile, in the evenings as we sat on the big front porch in the house we all grew up in, I was aware of his presence close to me. He made me feel safe.

"I'm seventy-eight years old now. My younger sister died about five years ago at the age of sixty-two. Lately she has been visiting me too, almost every night. Whenever I see her, she looks about eight years old. She's carrying her doll. I know it's her by the Buster Brown bobbed haircut we all wore back in those days and by the pink ribbon in her hair. She spends most of her time crouched on the carpet in front of my TV set, slowly rocking her baby doll.

"Whenever I go for a snack at bedtime, I call out to my brother and sister (I can see and hear them plain as day, even though I can only feel the presence of my dear mother at my side), 'Anyone for ice cream, or cookies and milk?' They don't answer me, but they make a lot of noise on their own, just to let me know that they are here, keeping me company. But nobody rushes to the kitchen with me, so I believe I have learned one thing about my gentle ghosts, or my family angels, if you prefer to call them that. It's just this: They have no real bodies, at least not on visits to earth.

"I wonder if God lets angels come to earth at their favorite age, or at the age at which they can do the most good in the assignment they have been given. I wonder. Sometimes I awaken to hear my mother's laughter, as well as the noises of my brother and sister. I will turn to say something to my mother, only to find that she has disappeared. I also used to look for my older sister to talk to, as she was the most fun of any of my family. But so far she hasn't shown up. Maybe she is busy elsewhere.

"I am comforted to think that if God sent my mother to me because I cried out for her, then she was evidently supposed to give me encouraging thoughts about this sickness of mine. So I thank you, God, for my mother. And for the presences of my sister and brother too. I feel like they have moved in for the duration. Sometimes I feel selfish if I eat in front of them. Once I said loudly as I walked out of the kitchen with my cereal I had fixed for breakfast, 'Help yourself.' But there was no answer. Yet I know they are loving and protecting me. Sometimes they go away for a day or two, but then they come back.

"Now I understand the phrase in 1 Corinthians, 'Now we see through a glass darkly, but soon we shall see face to face.' So I have been blessed. The promise is there. Soon I will see them face to face. I will see them and we will embrace one another. So I am comforted by my gentle ghosts."

It is just as easy to believe in gentle ghosts than in fierce, terrifying hauntings. And if the gentle family ghosts of the past can come into our present awareness, they can help you and me, as they helped my elderly friend, to prepare for the future. They can both comfort and console us. If there is indeed no time and no space where angels are concerned, then my friend's gentle family angels can and will continue to surround her with their loving presence and guide her safely home into her dear mother's arms.

CHAPTER TEN

THE MIRACLE OF DIVINE ORDER AND SYNCHRONICITY

*When you ask for guidance and assistance, simply assume
that it immediately is pouring forward.... Live in the total assumption
that the moment you ask for guidance it is pouring in.*

—GARY ZUKAV

The Library Angel

Books, with their secret knowledge, free me from myself....
The greatest minds in history wait by my bed, sit patiently
in bookcases, respond to my touch. I reach out and they
are there, waiting to transport me to another realm.

—LINDA WELTNER

Even logical, rational, scientific, academic people have access to angels. Here is a story that was told me by not one, but two different people, one a college professor, one a writer. I asked each of these individuals to tell me about miracles in their lives, and as is often the case at first, they each told me that there were no miracles in their ordered, rational lives.

"Except," said the professor, "of course you've heard about the library angel."

This sounded interesting. "Tell me more."

."Well, of course everyone knows about the library angel," he insisted. "Anyone who has ever prepared for their dissertation, anyone who's ever had to prepare a syllabus for class or do research for a journal. You go along with your accustomed discipline, pulling together snippets and bits from the main scholars in your field, until —"

"Until?" I prompted.

"Well, I really can't speak for anyone else. Maybe I'm just lucky, or tuned in, or, conversely, desperate enough to ask the help of the library angel. But what happens is this: You've come to the end of your usual sources, and you're in the library, usually late at night before the paper or the class or the abstract is due. And you can't find anything. Anything else to add, I mean. And that's when you whisper to the library angel, 'Help me!' And then you run your hands along the stacks of books, and something always happens."

"What?"

"The library angel comes to your rescue. A book falls off the shelf onto your head. A book opens into your hands at exactly the right page. I swear I have been sitting at the carrel when a book I didn't even know existed sailed onto the desktop and fluttered its pages until it fell open, with a sort of sigh of satisfaction, to exactly the right information I was looking for."

I asked him if it happened to him all the time.

"More and more," he admitted. "It seems like the more I allow myself to accept the possibility that a library angel exists, the more she is there to help me."

"She?" I asked in disbelief. "Is the library angel a she?"

"Well, absolutely," he declared. "I can almost see her long, flowing robes between the stacks. And her hands are long and narrow and precise. She's what they used to call a muse, someone to help the scholar with his work."

I asked another writer friend if she too had experienced the library angel.

"Definitely," she said. "It started when I was a little girl and had decided to read every book in the public library. Well, that was obviously impossible. So I would sneak into the adult section at the big Carnegie Library downtown, and I would run my hands along the shelves, up as high as I could reach, and whatever books wanted to be read by me would fall into my outstretched hands. Then when I was a teenager I thought I could just go into the library and sort of sniff and be led to the right section and the right books. Later I got more sophisticated with it. Now I'll go into my own library at home, and I'll just ask my very own library angel — everyone who works with words has one, I believe, although maybe he or she doesn't know it yet — anyway, I'll just ask, and pretty soon here comes the book that has the quotation I want. Sometimes it's even hidden in a section behind other books. Sometimes I've forgotten that I even bought, much less read, the book.

"I remember one day, it was just the most amazing thing! I had been searching for a way to tie in the theme of a chapter I was writing together with the narrative, and I needed something — anything! — a quotation, an idea, you name it, to make it all work. Well, I was pacing up and down and muttering to myself and I happened to stop in front of one of my seven-foot bookcases. You have to understand that there are three rows of books in that one bookcase alone. The stacks run two deep, and then a front stack is shelved sort of catty-cornered face-out, for the books I have written or else use all the time. All of a sudden, behind the highest stack, well above my head, from the back row of the third layer deep, comes this book sailing out of nowhere! It even knocked over several books in its way in its eagerness to get to me. And it was, of course, the perfect book that I needed at the time, one I had hauled all over the country for years and never even gotten around to reading. And there it was! It was the first time, though certainly not the last time, that my library angel cooperated with my need.

"Sometimes, when I'm very tense and on deadline, I swear that there are books flying all over the place. I just have to be willing to receive them into my hands. I learn to stand out of the way when this happens, because a few times a lot of books have fallen down after being shoved, I guess, by the book struggling to get my attention. So now I'm more careful. I ask for what I want, and then I carefully lift off any books in the way until the book I want pops into my awareness and then into my hands."

"But why do you call that experience a library angel?"

"Listen, I have thousands of books. Without a library angel, I'd never know which one was exactly the right one for me to open that day to find the information I need."

The library angel seems to be useful for more than finding books, pages, research, quotations, and so on. My friend went on to tell me that she is so in love with books that they come flying to her in a bookstore as well.

"I've saved a lot of money by simply asking my library angel — well, maybe you could call her a bookstore angel as well — to guide me to the perfect book that I need to buy next."

We were standing in my favorite bookstore as we chatted, and on impulse I asked the owner of the bookstore if she had ever heard of the library angel or the bookstore angel.

"Of course," she said. "I love books, but I probably would never have thought of having a bookstore of my own except that —" she hesitated. "This is going to sound strange."

We reassured her that we had heard everything.

"Well," she said. "Books just keep coming to me. Hundreds and thousands of books, old and new. But after I retired from the school system, I wanted a bookstore of my own. And I knew what a risk it was, and how little money you could make — you know, all the things they teach you in a basic entrepreneurial workshop. But I kept on getting nudges from something, someone, well, I guess you could call it my bookstore angel. Because books kept on showing up in my life by the barrelful. If I gave away ten books to friends, a hundred more poured into my life. Like coat hangers, my own books seemed to just multiply whenever I wasn't looking. I didn't have room. So I went in with a friend who had a small bookstore and some meeting rooms for workshops. And I've been here ever since. But if the books hadn't started flowing into my life, as if they were flung by a mysterious hand, maybe I wouldn't have taken the chance. My life is filled to overflowing with books and their incredible, fascinating contents. And I do think that there was a bookstore angel involved.

"There's another thing that she helps me with," continued the bookstore owner. "I can always — and I mean always! — locate just the book the customer wants. Just by osmosis, I guess. Or maybe my bookstore angel continues to help me. Everyone who comes into the store remarks about this. And hardly anyone ever leaves without a book or two or three, exactly what the person wanted. I thank my bookstore angel every day for that."

So of course my friend and I bought books, wonderful books, from the owner before we left.

"Now I'll have to find a place for these," my friend concluded. "I'll have to get rid of more of my books. Guess I'll call on the library angel again. The library angel is wonderful to help you when you want to give books to others or simply cull the overflowing shelves. She guides me in the decision-making process. Oh no," she said fervently, "I couldn't do without my library angel."

I remembered my first spiritual teacher telling me, "Beyond the visible is the invisible." Here was a perfect example. I've gotten in touch with my own library angel recently. It makes my work so much easier. And it's great to have someone go before you, flowing robes and all, picking out the books you need with her precise, long-fingered, artistic hands. Sometimes I almost see her, if it's a cloudy day or at night. But even when I don't, I thank my lucky stars for my library angel, who is helping me even as I write this book.

Missed Planes and Divine Timing

Miracles result from our recognition that even the worst news
is only a short story; the whole plot is an unfolding mystery.
Be humble in your perpetual uncertainty.

—PAUL PEARSALL

A dear friend of mine has experienced more miracles, more amazing coincidences, and more powerful manifestations of divine order at work in his life than anyone I can recall. Every time I meet with him, he tells me of another mystical encounter, another instance of serendipity, another rescue. Here is one of his favorite stories. He calls it his "divine timing" story.

"Years ago, when I lived on Cape Cod, my best friend and I, who both worked in the medical profession, were going together to a medical conference in Boston. I don't know how familiar you are with that part of the country, but we always allowed ourselves about an hour and a half to get to the airport, plus another half-hour to forty-five minutes for check-in and any delays we might encounter.

"It was a beautiful day, and we started out, for some reason or another, with extra time to spare. In fact, we had about three hours before the plane was due to take off, so my friend and I decided on a leisurely drive, with a stop or two along the way. We had both worked very hard lately, and we enjoyed the long drive and each other's conversation.

"Well lo and behold, as we meandered along, we came to first one detour and then another. There was a lot of road construction going on. But we just laughed about it all, and decided it was time to 'take the road less traveled by,' and so we didn't let the detours or the delay bother us one bit. Later on, when we were at last back on the main highway, we were slowed to a halt again because of a truck that had jackknifed off the highway. After stopping to ascertain if anyone had been hurt and being told by the police in charge to just move along, we did so. We still had lots of time, and so when we discovered that we had a flat tire we even joked about that too, although it took some time to put on the temporary spare and limp along to the nearest service station. We had meant to stop for lunch along the way, but now we suddenly found that our time was running short, so we decided to push on to the airport. Further construction and an unbelievable traffic jam on the way to the airport slowed us even more. We couldn't believe our luck!

"When we finally made it to the airport, we both realized that the plane would be leaving in just a few minutes and we didn't have time to park the car.

" 'You go ahead and catch the plane,' I urged my friend. 'I'll park in the outlying lot and catch the next flight. Go on. Don't worry about me!'

"So we unloaded his bags hastily, and he set off for a trot down the long corridors to his gate. By the time I had wrestled the car into an out-of-the-way parking space, I was exhausted. I went back to the main terminal and decided to have a bite to eat before even trying to get on the next plane. I knew I had missed our originally scheduled flight, but I figured that my friend had made it in time after all.

"Shaking my head at the unexpected and unbelievable delays along our three-hour journey, I had just settled down in the coffee shop when I saw the tall figure of my friend come loping toward me, a grin on his face. 'I could have made the flight,' he said. 'I still had three minutes. But I decided, what the heck — I would wait for you and we could take the next flight together.'

"Delighted, I asked him to sit down and we continued our conversation, joking and laughing at all the delays. Pretty soon a waitress came to take our order. She seemed very upset, so we asked her what was wrong.

" 'Didn't you hear?' she asked. 'What a shame! What a horrible tragedy! That last flight to Boston just went down. Just twelve minutes out of the airport. They don't know the details yet. They don't know yet how many people survived the crash. But they are not hopeful. Too early to notify the families. But it looks bad.' She shook her head. 'Good thing you were not on that flight,' she told us. And then, 'May I take your order?'

"We both just sat there in total shock and numbness. The enormity of what we had just escaped finally set in, and we both began trembling with shock and fatigue. Later, we learned that no one had survived. We never did find out what had caused the crash.

"My friend had waited for me instead of getting on that flight. And together we had been stopped, slowed, delayed, detoured again and again until there was no possibility of getting on that particular plane. We don't know why it happened that way. We don't know why we were spared and the other passengers went down. It's a mystery.

"We both decided to skip the next commuter flight to Boston and canceled our medical conference reservations. We went back to my car and drove slowly home. It only took us a little over an hour, instead of almost three. We were both very quiet on the way home. There was no way to figure out the mystery of why we had both been spared.

"We were friends for years, until I left that part of the country and moved out west. But I have never forgotten my friend's smiling face as he ran over to my table and announced, 'I thought I'd wait and go with you.' Thank God he did!

"I don't get too perturbed at any delays in my life now. I figure that they are there for a reason, and I'd better not lean against the universe in order to speed up my path through time. I just call it 'the miracle of divine timing' and let it go at that."

A Writer's Fairy Tale

*If we had to say what writing is, we would define it
essentially as an act of courage.*

—CYNTHIA OZICK

This chapter would not be complete without a miraculous writer's tale. I like
to call it a "once upon a time" tale, because of its mysterious fairy tale quality.
If you make your living in the arts, you can easily substitute artist, sculptor, ac-
tor, or dancer for the protagonist in this real-life fairy tale.

Once upon a time there lived a writer who had written and published
many books, but whose life had taken a downturn for several years. The books
she had previously published were not selling. The book she had worked on
for two years and already sold was canceled. And the book projects she was
currently working on were going nowhere. Both her livelihood and her sanity
were at stake.

So one day she decided to ask her writing angel for help. Now all arti-
sans have a special angel, separate and distinct from their guardian angel, who
watches over them and helps to shape their creative work. Or so my friend believed. And what you believe, more often than not, comes true. And since my
friend was a good, disciplined, professional writer who had a lot more to say,
she decided that she needed spiritual help to open publishing doors for her.

She prayed for the perfect agent, the perfect editor, the perfect publisher, and the perfect book project to materialize in her life. Then she got back to her current projects while waiting for the answers to her prayers.

For awhile nothing happened. Then one day a woman she had never met, a friend of another writing friend, called her long-distance from across the country. It was one of those "out of the clear blue sky" calls. The woman who called became a good friend of the writer, and even asked her to travel east to share a vacation home on the shore with her and the writer's original friend. So she did, although money was tight and discouragement a daily companion.

"Well, if I'm going to spend all that money, I might as well attempt to interest some agents in my book projects," she reasoned, and sent off letters announcing her visit to New York State, requesting that interviews be set up. Lo and behold, several agents responded, expressing an interest in a preliminary meeting. But because of time and location constraints (the writer was to stay several hours away from the agents' offices in Manhattan), she was able to arrange only one firm meeting, and that one contingent on complicated time and travel arrangements that would have to dovetail perfectly on one specific day.

My writer friend, normally a resourceful and strong individual, fell victim to a bus breakdown and arrived breathlessly late at the meeting, where she promptly and unprofessionally burst into tears. The agent, a wise and motherly woman, fed her and soothed her and listened to her story of projects canceled and books unsold. Then she told my friend that she would represent her, on the strength of her past publications and her current writing skills. So that was a miracle right then and there, and not a minute too soon, and not the first one either, if you count the serendipitous original phone call and the vacation trip.

And so my writer friend went home and rewrote and revised everything she could think of, which was a considerable amount of work because she had been writing and sometimes publishing for over twenty years. She also had a number of new ideas and book proposals to write as well. But nothing happened for a long time. Isn't that always the way, just when you think miracles are going your way?

Just to cheer herself up my writer friend began to take long early morning and early evening walks, and every time she did so she would come back with inspirational stories that popped into her head, again from out of the clear blue sky, fully formed and rather revealing of the writer's own trials and tribulations and triumphs, but definitely and positively unsaleable. Or so she thought. She wrote down a few of them anyway, just in case, and went on with her commercial projects.

Months later, my friend's agent, at wit's end at not being able to interest New York publishers in her work, sent a series book proposal to a smaller but well-respected California publisher. They were unsure about the potential of the project, but the day before they sent the book series back to the agent, a colleague of the writer, a woman she had not seen or spoken to for years, just happened to be visiting the offices of the California publisher. And while there, she just happened to see, on the publisher's desk, the name of the writer on the material being sent back.

"I know her!" she exclaimed, or something like that, and went on to tell the publisher that she had always wanted to work with that particular writer. But not with that series, not with that project.

And lo and behold the California publisher offered the writer's colleague a partnership, and lo and behold the writer's long-lost colleague called the struggling writer she had lost touch with and demanded to see what else the writer had written. And lo and behold the writer just happened to have the inspirational stories she had been given — I swear! — by her writing angel in her walks, and so she sent the ten stories she had, although everyone knows that personal inspirational essays are a hard sell, and lo and behold the colleague bought and published them, with many more added on. And one day the writer realized that in one year's time, give or take a couple of months, she had indeed found the perfect agent, the perfect editor, the perfect publisher, and the perfect book project.

And they all lived and worked and published happily ever after, with the help, of course, of the writing angel.

And *that's* divine order and synchronicity!

CHAPTER ELEVEN

THE MIRACLE OF GREAT CHANGE

To battle a demon is to embrace it, to face it
with clarity of vision and humility of the heart....
These demons, these parts of us that haunt us, torture us,
and reduce us, are the agents of change. They throw down
the gauntlet to the warrior within us to face them in a duel.

—*STEPHANIE ERICSSON*

Andy and Addiction

*When you struggle with addiction, you deal directly with
the healing of your soul. You deal directly with the matter of your life....
This is the work of evolution. It is the work you were born to do.*

—GARY ZUKAV

Nowhere is forgiveness more required than of those souls who struggle with addiction. For stories about the miracles that come into the lives of those in recovery, I went to a man who has been there and back in his own life.

"Every person I have ever met in recovery has a miracle story to tell," he assured me. "For it is only when we cannot go on, when we are out of control, when we hit bottom or pretty near, that miracles can occur to change our lives around."

"But *how* exactly do they occur?" I asked, not having been involved in the recovery movement myself, but knowing people who had.

"You know that old saying, 'God knocks us to our knees so we can pray?'" he asked me. "That's what happens in the recovery movement, especially in AA."

"Okay," I said. "Give me an example."

"How many do you need?" he asked me.

And then he told me this amazing story of the most down-and-out, hopeless drunk he had ever met.

"Seems that this guy, let's call him Andy, lived in a one-room, piss-poor apartment, subsisting on a disability allowance from the government. He couldn't work, and his mind was as screwed up as his physical life. He was dirty and smelly and when he got on a bus — which is what he did, he rode buses all day long and into the night, and tried to talk to the people on the bus or cadge a handout from them — well, you could have known he was in your area a block away, just by his smell. Everyone avoided him, of course, and looked right through him as though he didn't exist, even though he would get in your face if he could. One night it got so bad on a nighttime bus ride that the driver threw him off into the snow. Just couldn't have him upsetting the other passengers.

"Well, he told me this story about that night, and I swear it's true. He stumbled through the snow back to his apartment — limping and bruised from the fall from the bus and cursing a blue streak. It was cold and dark, and he could hardly see his way because of the snow. He finally made his way back to the parking lot in front of his one-room apartment. He was mumbling and weaving around, trying to fit his key into the lock, when he heard a voice. It said, 'Andy!' Just that one word, calling his name. He whirled around, but there was no one there. Of course he was drunk and wet and cold and exhausted, so he thought maybe he was just hearing things. Then the voice called his name again: 'Andy!' And he told me that there was such a timbre to that voice, he couldn't explain it, such a presence, that he whirled around again and dropped his key. The voice called a third time, 'Andy!' and then added, 'Look over here.'

"He straightened up and looked in the direction the voice commanded. And he saw a light. He swore later that it was a white light, whiter than the snow, a light unlike any he had ever seen. And the light was warm, while the snow was cold. And he couldn't stand up to the light. He literally fell to his knees. And he told me that he felt such peace, such kindness, such love from this white light that had materialized before him that he literally couldn't move. He was just immersed in that light. And after a long while, the light just sort of faded away, and the presence within the light went too.

"And Andy said that he knelt in the snow a long time, not thinking or cursing, just holding that knowingness of the light. And then he got up, found his key, went into his one-room hovel, and bathed himself. After that he cleaned up his apartment. Then he took his clothes to the Laundromat. And then he got a shave and a haircut. And ate breakfast. And started looking for a job.

"And, according to Andy, he never drank again from that moment on. He went to AA meetings, he told his story again and again, and every time he told it you could feel the energy and the emotion. He didn't know why the light had come to him and not to someone else, someone more deserving, or so he thought. He didn't know how the light had known his name. Or why the light cared at all. But that experience changed him in one moment. And he's been changed ever since."

Sleeping Beauty and the Great Change Artist

We move in life from the unconscious perfection of childhood,
to the conscious imperfection of middle life,
to the conscious perfection of old age.

—*Marion Woodman*

Stories of addiction can shift to stories of amazing change. I interviewed a woman who told me the ongoing, wonderful story of what I call "Sleeping Beauty and the Great Change Artist."

The story originally began with the woman's stepmother dying. At least, everyone thought she was. She was a loving woman, who had been feeble for some time, had a seizure, and lapsed into a coma. The family kept vigil for a month before accepting the need to let go and call her son to come from New York to California to say good-bye to his mother. Finally, after thirty days, they reluctantly gave permission for the mother's feeding tube to be disconnected. As her son from New York walked into the room, expecting to say a last good-bye to a comatose and dying woman, his mother woke up! She looked at him and said, "Good morning," very calmly.

Amazingly, she began to get better, and while doctors cautioned that in her semivegetative state she could go at any time, there were more and more periods of lucidity. Once, her stepdaughter came to say her last good-byes. Instead, the dying woman carried on an hour-long conversation with her!

Meanwhile, my friend's father was having his own great period of adjustment. He had buried two wives, and now his third wife was leaving too. As I interviewed his daughter, she explained to me that he had been married to her mother (his second wife) for thirty-five years before she died. He then looked up his first wife (whom he had originally left to marry my friend's mother) and joined her in the country of her birth. They intended to travel home to the United States so that she could meet his children, and then they were going to formalize their reunion.

"But his first wife died suddenly of heart failure just two days before my father's visa expired," explained the daughter. "When he got back home, he was just ripped apart — this new loss happened just two years after my mom died. He moved into an apartment alone for the first time in his life, and then was lucky enough to meet a wonderful woman, who is now my stepmother."

I was fascinated by the story of this long-lived man who had loved and lost so many times. But there was more to come.

At eighty-one years of age, this man was rigid and irascible. Because of a severe hearing loss and his refusal to be fitted for a hearing aid, his days were even more frustrating. Add to that the fact that he was a lifelong drinker and smoked three packs of cigarettes a day. In addition, he was virtually immobile, due to a stroke three years previously that had partially paralyzed his left side.

Now his beloved third wife was in the hospital. He had cared for her for several years, ever since a tumor had been successfully removed from her brain. He had watched over her with his own decreasing, alcohol-impaired judgment. Taking care of her was his primary therapy after his own stroke. As he became increasingly unable to function well in other areas of his life, these activities became even more important to him. When his wife was admitted to the hospital, his entire *raison d'etre,* his role and his importance, disappeared. He was unbearably lonely and found it difficult to function. His entire world was turned upside down.

Then the money ran out. The fiercely independent and grieving old man was faced with a need to move, as their only asset was a house they had lived in for many years. The obvious solution was a nursing home, but the old man was adamant in rejecting that option. He had lost all his previous points of reference and had nothing familiar in his life left to cling to. Nevertheless, the house had to be sold.

All the man had left was his love for his dying wife. So he opted for a retirement home where he hoped that he would be able to go and visit her occasionally. Finally, miracle of miracles, he was accepted in a dual facility, one in which he could live in the retirement portion of the home and his wife could be cared for in the skilled nursing section. He could see her every day and have that much more time with her.

But this eighty-one-year-old man could not adjust to the loss of his accustomed life. He was so abusive to the staff that within a week the director of the retirement home warned him that he must leave if he could not change. He had nowhere else to go. His options had run out. He had come face to face with the consequences of every habit that had sustained him over his long life. He had to change or die.

He changed. First came the removal of his long-standing addictions. He quit both smoking and drinking cold turkey. No one thought that he could do it, but he wanted one last chance at life.

Next came a request for a hearing aid. His frustration with not understanding and not being able to be understood by others was changing as well. Next he asked for a word processor. Many years earlier, this once creative and charming man had written a book. It was a collection of letters to his second wife (the one of thirty-five years, the one whose daughter I had interviewed) about her and their life together. He had written the book after her death, as at that time only two things mattered to him — his emotions and his writing. Although he made his living in other ways, writing was his creative outlet. Now he wanted to chronicle and communicate his life in writing.

According to his daughter, "Writing on a computer about his emotions is his way of communicating with the world. It validates his existence as a human being, when all the other evidence is that he is a nonentity without a home, without a partner, without mobility, living on a schedule determined by strangers, and watching his last, beloved wife die."

But this indomitable old man is anything but a has-been. Last seen, he was hunched over the computer, determined to learn a new skill so that he could write his life. Twice a day, this formerly enraged and enfeebled man visits his wife in her part of the facility. He is determined to be creative and alive to the very end of his life.

His daughter thought that this was an amazing story, and so do I. "You could say of my father that he was a great person with great faults. He should have been a professor with students that listened to his lectures. He should have been a success in some kind of intellectual area, where he could use his gifts. He thought of himself as a 'failed' writer. Yet here he is, at the very end of his days, writing. Using his mind, using his emotions, telling his life. Was there ever such a great change artist?"

The Course in Miracles states: "There is no order of difficulty in miracles." This man's life proves that this is true. So Sleeping Beauty and the Amazing Great Change Artist continue to live. Godspeed!

CHAPTER TWELVE

THE MIRACLE OF THE FUTURE

*In the depth of winter, I finally learned
that within me there lay an invincible summer.*

—*ALBERT CAMUS*

The Woman in the Purple Suit

I am trying to keep my soul alive in times not hospitable to soul.

—J. M. COETZEE

One of the more intriguing stories I came across while interviewing both friends and strangers was the one I call "The Woman in the Purple Suit." Here is her story.

"This is a miracle that happened to me. It is one I cannot explain by rational means, nor any means at all.

"Several years ago, I had to make a heart-wrenching decision that would change my life forever. My business was overextended and underfinanced, and it was only a matter of a month or so when I would be forced to close and move elsewhere. This was a good business, a small business, built from nothing seven years previously. It was my entire life. I had poured all my energy, including my heart and my soul, into this tiny company. Yet I was caught up in a disastrous recession that only seemed to get worse the longer I hung on. I couldn't sleep. I was often exhausted and ill. I did not know what my future would be. I had constant insomnia.

"One night I got up and fixed myself a cup of tea and huddled, shivering, on the couch. My small apartment was attached to the offices where I conducted my business, so it seemed that there was no time when I could escape the decisions that had to be made and the work that had to be done. I was wide awake, and my mind moved in circles. Everything that I had created in the last seven years was bitter dust in my mouth.

"I know that I prayed then, as I had for a number of days and nights. I prayed for money, prayed for my business to be saved, prayed that I could pay my debts, prayed that I could start all over again. At some point in my prayers, I lay my head back against the sofa and subsided into quiet.

"It was then that I saw her: the figure on the other end of the couch. The woman in the purple suit.

"I sat up, startled, more awake than I can ever remember, my heart pounding in my chest. I could not say a word. I could only stare at the woman in the purple suit.

"She was older than I was, by a few years or so. Her hair was a combination of silver and gold and swept back from her face. Her face — well, her face was beautiful. A porcelain complexion, wide, crinkly lines at the corners of her deep, kind eyes. She looked so wise, and so gentle, and yet so purposeful. A well-groomed, slightly plump, middle-aged woman sitting on the end of my couch. And she had on a purple suit. It was a shade between violet and periwinkle blue. The shade almost matched her eyes, which were blue and piercing and, while they were kind, seemed intelligent. I was intrigued by the buttons on her suit. They were of a silver that matched her hair, intricate circles with a strange design of chased silver within each one. They looked ancient. She looked real. In fact, she looked just like a prosperous business-woman who had come to conduct a meeting.

"She smiled at me. Her smile washed over me like waves of light, like waves of love. It was a smile of such intimacy and concern that I wanted to crawl into her lap and cry. But I understood that we were not to touch one another, even though I reached out my hand.

" 'It will be all right,' she said softly. 'It will all be all right.'

"Immediately a dozen questions rushed to my lips, but I did not speak.

"She placed one well-manicured finger on her lips to indicate silence.

" 'Who are you?' I managed to blurt out. She merely smiled. 'You know who I am,' she said softly.

" 'Are you an angel?' I blurted out.

" 'I am your future self,' she said. 'I am your best, your highest self. And I have come to tell you that all will be well.'

" 'All will be well?' I repeated.

" 'Yes,' she said serenely. 'There is nothing to fear. Your future is secure. Your future is safe. All will be well.'

"And then she was gone. I blinked in surprise at the empty air at the end of the couch. All that was left was a sense of peace, of love, of serenity, of safety. I felt profoundly comforted. I went to bed then and slept soundly for the first time in weeks.

"I told only one friend about this strange encounter. He smiled at me.

" 'How fortunate you are,' he said, 'To be so loved by your future self.'

" 'But it was an angel, wasn't it?' I asked him. 'An angel in a purple suit?'

" 'Call it by whatever name you will,' he said. 'It was real. And the face looked like your own.'

" 'Like looking into a mirror,' I admitted. 'It was eerie. But more than me. Much more beautiful than me.'

" 'Who knows?' he said. 'Perhaps you have some years ahead of you to grow into that person.'

" 'Oh no,' I protested. 'It must have been an angel.'

"Almost immediately, or so it seemed, I moved away from the apartment attached to the offices. I moved to another part of the country. I came to terms with that time in my past when challenges forced me to let go of everything that I had accomplished and everything in my life that I had held dear. I started over.

"Often I looked for a purple suit, one with intricately designed silver buttons. I haven't found one. Not yet. Along the way, I grew older and plumper and I hope, wiser as well. My hair turned an interesting combination of silver and gold. I learned calmness. I became kinder.

"I tell myself that I can never become like the woman in the purple suit. For she was more than me. She was more beautiful, in her serenity and love, than I can ever be. But it's an image I can reach for, as I reached for the woman at the other end of the couch. And yes, everything is all right now. It's all come out all right. And my future is safe. My future is secure."

A Double Rainbow

We must be willing to get rid of the life we've planned,
so as to have the life that is waiting for us. The old skin
has to be shed before the new one can come.

—JOSEPH CAMPBELL

One morning when I was wrestling with some unresolved problems in my life, and wishing that I was anywhere in the world than where I was (a temporary state of affairs, since I am usually reasonably content with my home, my work, my life), the phone rang. The call was from a stranger in another state, a woman I had contacted several times with the hopes of an interview. An interview about miracles. She had one for me, and while she told me about it we both enjoyed the kind of rare, intimate, personal conversation that heralds the arrival of a new friend.

"I've been wanting to tell you my rainbow story," she began, "but it's only a little story. While it was a miracle of revelation to me, I'm not sure if it is a large enough miracle to qualify for your book."

I assured her that there were no measurements in miracles. In fact, as we talked, my own mood shifted from one of despair to quiet joy, a state of consciousness that steals upon me at rare moments unannounced.

"Here's the background for my miracle story," she told me. "Some years ago, I moved into an old Victorian house in Grass Valley, two hours from the San Francisco Bay Area. I moved there originally to repair a second marriage in its twelfth year. Interestingly enough, the old Victorian house and its attached three-fourths of an acre of land were in a state of disrepair as well. I thought I could reclaim the land into a garden. And so I did. I thought I could repair and renovate the house. But I had neither the money or the skills for that enterprise. Most of all, I wanted to repair my marriage. But that was impossible. We said good-bye after fourteen years.

"In order to counteract the emotions engendered by the divorce, I immediately flung myself into a new relationship. And I also continued to create the most beautiful garden imaginable on my property. Even while I was doing this, the third marriage, begun in such hope, flared and died.

"Oh, I felt so desolate, so despairing then! Most of all, there was a sense of failure. And deep anger. Emotionally, I finally came to terms with the fact that there was no Prince Charming to take care of me. That there never would be. Once and for all, I would have to take care of myself in every possible way. This was a liberating feeling, although accompanied by much inner pain as I strove to put the past into perspective and to rebuild my life. To do so, I turned again to my garden.

"Oh, it was magnificent! There was a hundred-year-old chestnut tree at the back of the property, a tree which had miraculously escaped the blight that had come into the area a few years previously and decimated most of the trees. This tree arched over the north side of the house from the backyard and provided a magnificent view as I seated myself daily beneath its sheltering branches and looked toward the house. I had reclaimed old rosebushes that now bloomed fragrantly from early April to mid-November. The house was falling down around me, with buckets poised at strategic places under the roof to catch the storms that poured through its shacklike exterior. But I had my garden. At least I had my garden.

"Yet the house had been the scene of so much inner devastation and pain in my life that I felt exhausted by the house's needs. I had no capital for the major improvements it required. It was the site of my deepest emotions, my deepest struggles. Yet I loved the house. I loved the garden even more. I was facing a dilemma. I needed money, I couldn't possibly repair my Victorian home, and yet I had my garden, my incredible, life-affirming garden. And so I stayed. For years I stayed, although off and on I contemplated leaving.

"One cool day in September, in the late afternoon before sunset, sitting out by the pool under the Chestnut tree and looking toward the back of the house, musing yet again on what to do, I raised my eyes past the outlines of the house.

"And I saw a double rainbow. It was a full-spectrum rainbow, with every color imaginable, and it shimmered in front of me and arched completely over both the house and the garden. Just a minute before I had been angry and despairing, feeling yet again that my life was a shambles, feeling yet again that I didn't know what to do, searching for signs and portents. Now, I was galvanized into action. I sprang to my feet and watched, openmouthed, as the rainbow seemed to move. It continued out of the garden. It continued past the house. In short, the double rainbow did more than span my house and garden and me with the sweep of its colors. It continued *beyond* my house and garden. The rainbow arched out into the world. It showed me the way out.

"At that moment these thoughts came to me, as if the rainbow had spoken. Before I had been saying to myself, 'How can I give up this garden? How can I leave it?'

"Now the answer came. 'If the garden exists in your heart, you can carry it with you wherever you go.'

"I listened for more answers. The rainbow continued shimmering, beckoning, arching out into the world. A rainbow path for me to follow.

"I thought to myself, with a quiet and pensive finality, 'It's okay to give up what I once had in order to get what I want now.'

"And what did I want? The answers rushed out from my heart as if they were solid physical things. 'I want love, I want intimacy, I want a caring mate, I want a beautiful relationship.' And then the next words popped into my mind: 'I want to be free of this house.'

"Next day, I called a local real estate agent. She listed the house and garden for what seemed to me to be an extremely high price, more than they were worth. At least to me. Yet the house sold in three days! Now that was a miracle!

"I moved back to Berkeley. In February, I met the dear man I am now married to. The double rainbow led me to where I wanted to be. Into another home. Into another life. With no regrets. And that was a miracle to me."

Is it possible that messengers from the future can come to us at the darkest moments of our lives? I believe this to be true. I have talked to many, many people who say, in essence, that something or someone, some sign, some dream, some promise of the good to come, came into their lives at a time when all else failed them. Whether a fortuitous phone call, whether a book that falls open to a page with a message that guides you onward, whether a double rainbow or a woman in a purple suit, at some moment or another we have all been led forward, gently, into our best future. Guidance takes many and varied forms. As does each miracle that leads us home.

CHAPTER THIRTEEN

THE MIRACLE OF GREAT DIFFICULTY

*You gain strength, courage, and confidence by every experience
in which you really stop to look fear in the face....
You must do the thing you think you cannot do.*

—ELEANOR ROOSEVELT

A Mantra for Mom

I suspect we are all recipients of cosmic love notes.
Messages, omens, voices, cries, revelations, and appeals
are homogenized into each day's events.

—SAM KEEN

Can you get through life without bumps and bruises, obstacles and obstructions, struggles and tests? Can you get through life without loss? You might as well ask if you can get through life without experiencing life. You may as well imagine that you can get through life without experiencing death. No matter how much we think that our lives can or should or must be an unending upward continuum of ever-increasing success, that's not what we are here for. While we look for joy, while we sort out and overcome old character patterns, while we learn who we are and what contribution we can make to the world, life happens. And it is not neat and tidy. And it is not perfect. And it never will be.

Sometimes life hands us great difficulties. And that's when our greatest learning begins. Perhaps your greatest difficulty looks like a mere hangnail to me. Perhaps I cannot even conceive of the pain you must be experiencing with your greatest difficulty.

A friend of mine with both an autistic child and a normal child lost her bright, loving child in a car accident. She rocked herself and her autistic child back to some semblance of normality, even as her marriage crumbled and her life changed beyond recognition.

"Here is my miracle story," she told me.

"When my first son, Brian, was born, he was such an incredible little being. I felt a love for him and a bond with him that I had never felt before. I knew somehow that his purpose here on earth was to show me what love is and make me feel that my essence was being cherished. He was just such a sunny light to everyone, including his younger brother, Alex, who was born with severe mental and emotional problems. I love Alex so much, yet because of his severe bipolar disorder, learning difficulties, physical difficulties, and what we later learned was a slight autism, Alex needed me constantly, night and day, to help make his world manageable. I remember rocking him night after night for years. I never slept at all in those years.

"But Brian was such a ray of light. Once, when he knew how exhausted I was with taking care of Alex's needs, Brian wrote what he called 'A Mantra for Mom.' He put it on the refrigerator while I was gone one day.

"This is what it said: 'I love Mom. You're terrific. You're pretty. You're nice. You're tough. You're strong. You're a safe, strong woman. You're a good mom. You're superwoman.'

"He told me that he put it on the refrigerator so that I would know how much he loved me while he was away at school.

"The boys were very close. They were immersed in Star Wars and all its games and collectibles. Brian and Alex would play for hours in Brian's room, and Alex always seemed better, more conscious, after his play hours with Brian.

"One day, shortly after Brian had put the 'Mantra for Mom' on the refrigerator, he rode his bike as usual to school. I remember his sunny smile and his hug (he loved hugging people), his arms around my neck before he left.

" 'Bye, Mom!' he said, 'I love you and I'll see you soon.'

"That was the last time I saw him alive. A car hit Brian on his way to school and killed him instantly.

"I remember when I came home, the first thing I saw was the 'Mantra for Mom' on the refrigerator.

"I went through the grieving process for what seemed like years. My marriage crumbled under the strain. And then I began to study and train how I could help other parents with their losses. Only after you go through the loss of a child can you help others in similar circumstances. I had been a part-time nurse. Now I became a trained spiritual counselor.

"Now you may wonder what the miracle is in all of this. Well, Brian's death did more than change me, change my path of service, change my healing purpose.

"It changed Alex as well. Alex could never bear to be touched, except for the rocking that went on each night from the time he was born. One day, when I came home from work, Alex pointed to the words that Brian had left on the refrigerator. Then he smiled and ran to me and gave me a big hug. This was so unexpected and so loving that tears came to my eyes. From that time on, Alex, as if sensing the need I had for love, began to reach out his arms more to me every day. In between school and supper, he would go into Brian's room and play with the Star Wars toys, especially Yoda, as if Brian was still there and was playing with him. He would talk to Brian. So this second child, who could not express his feelings, tolerate hugs, nor give love, gradually incorporated those gifts from his brother into himself. It was as if Brian was still there, teaching Alex how to love and care and function in the physical world.

" 'Alex loves Mom,' was one of the first remarkable things he said to me. But more remarkable things were to follow. Alex began to learn, began to socialize, began to relate to others. It was a long process. Now Alex is ready for college. His bipolar disorder is under control, his physical problems have almost disappeared, and he is a fully functioning, loving, caring young man.

"There is such a miracle in this that I cannot fully express it in words. Alex is Alex, he is *not* Brian. But it is as if his older brother's love taught him to love. Earlier, I said something that someone might think of as odd. I talked about how Brian made me feel that my very essence was cherished. That's how Alex makes me feel too.

"All my ideas about death have changed. Actually, all my ideas about love have changed too. If you were to ask me now what I think about death, I would say to you that death is just another form of life. That death is just going back to God. We don't have to fear it. I know, I just know, that heaven is so beautiful, and Brian is there. I know I will see it someday with him."

So Brian's death was a tremendous awakening. Brian's death and Brian's continuing love has changed everyone in the family.

"Oh yes. One more thing. Brian's 'Mantra for Mom' isn't on the refrigerator door anymore. It is in a special place of honor in my counseling room so that everyone who comes into that room can feel the essence of Brian. And I can remind myself daily that love never dies."

She paused for a moment to collect her thoughts. "Out of my greatest difficulty came a new life for me and my remaining son," she told me simply.

Reflecting on Difficulty

*The moment of grace comes to us in the dynamics
of any situation we walk into. It is an opportunity that God sews
into the fabric of a routine situation. It is a chance to do something creative,
something helpful, something healing, something that makes one unmarked
spot in the world better off for our having been there.*

—LEWIS B. SMEDES

"Out of my greatest difficulty came_____." You fill in the blank.

Sometimes our greatest difficulty is not about death. For death can be a kind and valued friend when someone you love is suffering. In the next chapter we will learn more of this awesome and irrevocable part of our lives, and the intense and luminous lessons it has for those of us involved in its passage.

For me, the greatest difficulty has been watching and caring for a loved one who is chronically and terminally ill. This lesson has come to me more than once in my life. Even as I write these pages, here it is again. An awesome lesson for me to learn and relearn. This lesson may come to you too.

So what is a discussion on great difficulties doing in a book about opening to miracles? Because it is through our greatest difficulties that we grow more conscious, more aware, more loving, more caring, more wise. It is through our greatest difficulties that our hearts break open and our hands are used in service. It is through our greatest difficulties that our souls awaken and deepen.

And how do we begin to reflect on our difficulties so that they can be transformed? We hold our difficulties up to the light just as we hold a kaleidoscope up to the light. And as our varied, chaotic experiences form and reform before our eyes, we begin to see the pattern of the difficulties, the problem, the crisis, the catastrophe, the opportunity. We begin to see in new ways. We begin to see both the light and the lesson. We begin to see the pattern of our lives.

I believe that our very lives are a kaleidoscope, not a fixed line from birth to death. And a miracle or two or three or more can occur when you hold the kaleidoscope of your life up to the light and let all the patterns fall into place, watching as each color, each variegated shape, turns into a coherent, beautiful, exquisite, original, and unique design. Each and every one of your experiences has contributed to the overall pattern of wisdom, clarity, and love you bring to your life. Nothing is ever wasted. Each moment of suffering, each joy, each lesson, everyone and everything you have experienced, all contribute their wealth of energetic life experience to you. It takes great courage to see your life as a kaleidoscope. Just as it takes courage to recognize the daily miracles in your life.

Opening to miracles is opening to life and death and all points in between. Opening to miracles is opening to the best within us, even when the opening itself comes out of our greatest difficulty. No one wishes anything but joy and health for themselves and for their loved ones. We want safe passage and sunny skies. And yet, when your greatest difficulty comes to you, begs for entrance, will not be ignored, what will you do? You cannot run away from it. You can only embrace the difficulty, walk through it as consciously as you can, hold it up to the light, and let your heart break open. As it most surely will. And then the difficulty, your greatest difficulty, will be transformed. As you have opened to it, so have you opened to miracles.

Gabriel, Messenger of God

The more absolute death seems, the more authentic life becomes.

—JOHN FOWLES

I had tried for months to get an interview with a friend of my publisher, a man whose beautiful young son had contracted leukemia at the age of seven, and had, after receiving the best medical care—and thousands of prayers from strangers, family, and friends — enjoyed almost four years in remission.

But on the Sunday afternoon that I was finally able to talk with Phil, Gabriel's father, his voice broke as he attempted to tell me the story. "Gabriel just had some more tests on Friday," he told me. "He's just a little kid still. We thought he was all right. We thought the leukemia was arrested. Now we don't know. Now we can only wait and pray and hope.

"But that's not the whole story," he went on. "I'm a writer myself, and I've been wanting to tell our family's story for some time. We are living an ongoing saga. We are living. That's one thing I can tell you. We are living through this. And we have learned well, we're still learning — about God, about faith, about the resilience of the human spirit. About love. About reconciliation and redemption. Those are high-sounding words to tell the story of a little boy who got sick, so dreadfully sick, and what happened to his family for almost four years — what is still happening.

"You see, the day after the initial diagnosis, I went into the hospital room where my wife was with Gabriel. And I just sank down by the bedside. There was this helpless seven year old just lying there, asleep. And I called upon the powers of the universe to heal him. To heal my child!

"Prayer was all that was left to me. We had put him in the doctor's hands, but there was nothing else we could do. If I thought that walking on my hands and knees to New York City from Berkeley would do it, would help my child live, I would do it. Without any question. Without a doubt. But there wasn't any such thing I could do that would save him.

"Then again, with these new tests, I've been going through sixteen shades of emotion all at once. I've been asking for miracles, and finding them, within the crisis itself, through the love and support and prayers of all those around our family. I just keep on asking for mercy. When he went into surgery for the tests, we put him into the Creator's hands and pleaded for mercy — not for ourselves, but for him.

"It's funny, I've never been a churchgoing man. I haven't talked to God for many years. Not until this. It's like the old wartime saying, 'There are no atheists in foxholes.' Well I don't think there are any parents who don't pray for the deliverance of their child from suffering and death, either.

"I went years without uttering a prayer. Who can I call on? What power do I have as a man, a husband, a father, to save my son? There's nothing you can do beyond a certain point. So you pray.

"But let me tell you more about this beautiful young boy, my son. He is the catalyst for all of us. He's almost eleven years old now, right on the verge of puberty. And he has lived through these four years. We all have. With the prayers of thousands of strangers and hundreds of friends, we have lived through this.

"And do you want to know what the miracle is? Getting in touch with aliveness. Every moment alive is richer and sweeter. Every moment you have with your loved ones is a gift. I'm coming to see that life is not about not having problems, but *living* through the problems. With grace. With love.

"I just keep on asking for help, and I do receive. There is a profound mercy in the world within the context of what is, what's really going on. And I now believe that pain comes from resisting what is. Pain comes from resisting the truth of a situation, whatever it is. Knowing this doesn't necessarily make it any easier, but I'm learning that facing the situation as it is will help me deal with it. And the way it is *does* change.

"Six months after Gabriel's initial diagnosis and that first hospital stay, I began to let go of the fear a bit. I began creeping out of the shadows. Yet on some level you can never escape. Life itself is a terminal disease. That's what I think sometimes. No matter how well I confront the shadow, it is always there. After he finished his three years of treatment, we thought we could put all this behind us. Guess what? You can't. You continue to be depressed, angry, anxious, worried. You grieve for the loss of your child's innocence — and your own. You wait for the other shoe to drop. And you never know whether today is going to bring you grief or joy. The one thing we want most desperately — control — is the one thing we can't have. You have to admit that, in a certain sense, you're powerless.

"I haven't mastered all of this. I'm still learning, still groping my way to understanding. I do believe that everything comes with a lesson, a blessing. Of course, you don't see the blessing when you're feeling the pain. That's why they call it pain!

"But if my happiness depends on things being a certain way, then I'm in trouble. If my ability to function in this world is predicated on making deals with God, then I'm in trouble. The universe doesn't negotiate. Yet prayer sustains. You are entitled to ask for what you want from God. That was a pivotal moment in my life, when I knelt at Gabriel's bedside. Prayer is not confined to any single form or purpose. I even pray when I'm coaching the kids on my younger son's soccer team. Coaching kids is a prayer because it leads to the further unfolding of that child, the best possible good for a child. I now believe that every beneficent thought is a prayer. Sometimes I pray that I will remember humility and not judge. Sometimes I pray for a way to live. Now my whole life is a prayer. Every deed a prayer.

"Over the last week, since we learned Gabriel had to have these tests, I have asked everyone I know to pray for my son. I have asked for help everywhere. I got a note from two dear friends of mine, who prayed for us and found this passage from *The Liturgy of the Hours*: 'This child will be great in the eyes of the Lord, for the hand of the Lord will be with him.' This was just the most incredible spiritual and emotional sustenance. To think that thousands of people are praying for Gabriel — and coming up with *that*.

"So far it has been a medical miracle, and much more: it is a sustaining spiritual miracle.

"Gabriel himself is amazing. He wore a baseball cap into surgery that says 'No Fear.' How's that for an eleven year old kid teaching us courage?

"So, one thing for sure is, there have been miracles and lessons galore in all this. We are learning to love as a family in the deepest and most holy sense of the word. We struggle and fight and hurt and plod along, and try to make our way. Through it all we remain faithful to each other, we continue to love each other. We're not saints, and we're not the heroes people sometimes tell us we are, but we do have love. And I'll say this: I loved my family before this all started happening, but I never knew I could love them this *fiercely*.

"Someone told me that the name Gabriel means 'messenger of God.' And he is. He has been a messenger, a wakeup call for all of us. There is so much love and courage residing in that little body, residing in that soul. He has taught us all. His struggle, *our* struggle, has brought us all to life — has put us more deeply in touch with the Mystery."

I had lost a son several years earlier, and I remembered the lessons of love, prayer, acceptance, and faith that he had taught me. Your heart breaks open in love, and you are changed forever. You are deepened in some profound and irrevocable way. You can never look at the world or other people in quite the same way again. You are changed in your depths.

For Phil and his family, Gabriel is indeed a messenger of God. As Phil says so eloquently, "The miracle is in the practice and the presence of love."

CHAPTER FOURTEEN

THE MIRACLES OF
BIRTH AND DEATH

The purpose of life is exploration. Adventure. Learning.
Pleasure. And another step towards home.

—*EMMANUEL (PAT RODEGAST)*

The Mystery of Creation

Life is a series of natural and spontaneous changes.
Do not resist them — that only creates sorrow.
Let reality be reality. Let things flow naturally forward
in whatever way they like.

—*LAO TZU*

I went straight to the source for this interview, talking to a midwife who had delivered a number of babies and who was still awestruck at the miracle that lay within each birth. (You met her earlier, as she spoke eloquently of her own journey through unwanted birth to a rebirth of self-acceptance. Her own journey has taught her well.)

"How would you define a miracle?" was my first and most basic question to her. It's the one I often use to prime the thought processes of the people that I talk with. That one question began an eager exploration of the miracles she encountered daily, in her work and in her life.

Here is her story.

"I think of the miracles in my life as a shift in my perceptions, a change in the way I look at things. It's like a clearing within me, a deep clearing. I go deeper and deeper as each miracle comes into my life. Each miracle taps deeper into a core level of self that allows me to find that peace and tranquillity that I seek.

"And the miracle of birth is the most miraculous miracle of all. Because this is what I see during a birth, especially with first-time mothers. I see the mystery of creation as it unfolds before my eyes.

"The woman experiences a feeling about herself from this experience that nothing else could possibly give her. She sees that she's a creative force. She sees that being feminine is very powerful, that being feminine is very wonderful, and that giving birth is the most powerful feminine experience she can have. It's a depth of empowerment that she receives. And that is a miracle in itself.

"We are working here with the creation of life. And working with the creation of life doesn't just mean that a baby is born. It can mean the creation of plants and animals, even the creation of ideas. And each creation requires that same deep clearing process I mentioned before. Each clearing goes deeper and deeper into the soul of a woman, and each miracle gets deeper and more profound as well. So it's both a miracle and a mystery when a woman gives birth."

"Is there any particular time during delivery that is especially poignant or intense?" I questioned.

"Well, birth is a natural process, and that process can be an intense one. After dilation, but before a woman delivers her baby, she goes into a place not of this world, very hard to reach. Some midwives say that it's the relief that the brain's endorphins bring, but I think it's much more. It's an energy that just takes the woman away. I remember one instance where we needed the assistance of the mother urgently. We had to draw her back in from that place, back from that intense, endorphin-like energy. We watched the transition being made in her energy. Her energy drew back in, it contracted after great expansion, and then with the mother's help we were able to take an especially urgent situation, in terms of the baby, and turn the situation into a miracle with the help of the mother's energy.

"My work is a miracle in itself. I have been able to observe ultimate femininity. Through participating in this creation of life I have been able to find out where my true power lies. And this has happened even though I have not had a child myself. Yet.

"It's interesting to me that memories begin to emerge from the birth situation, both for the mother and for me. Labor brings memories up to the surface. Memories stored in the body, memories stored in our feelings, they all tend to come up during the birth process. I have learned to shift my perception and just allow my own memories to come up and just allow myself to learn through the birth process. I learn anew each time I see birth happening. This is miracle work for me!

"I believe that it's worthwhile to examine your own childhood issues before you have a child. For those issues will certainly come up during pregnancy and labor. In fact, lack of progress during labor often involves repressed childhood memories. The woman's body reacts to old trauma and shuts down during delivery. We often help women giving birth to cry through the old trauma as part of their delivery. The body knows old traumas. The body always knows! And in the birth process, it cannot repress, it must express. Old unresolved issues about childhood come up to be resolved, especially in the third trimester.

"Home-birth participants value their self and their child. They know that the body has its own natural rhythms and that you can do it on your own, instead of being manipulated by technology. It takes real courage for a home birth. Yet the bonding between family members creates the miracle of birth even as it brings great happiness to all. Even though the fathers sometimes can't handle the intensity, if they stick it out, instead of walking out of the room, they can be a part of the experience. They can be a part of the miracle. They can bond with their child. I don't even have the words to tell you how that feels, to watch the mother and the father and the child together from the first breath of life onward. I keep on using the word miracle. There's no other word for it. And I am blessed to be a part of that process, again and again and again.

"All this has taught me a number of important lessons. One of these lessons is about struggle and surrender. Because watching the birthing process you have great opportunities to learn. We often struggle to get a miracle or make a miracle happen. This doesn't work. Let go of the struggle and *let* it happen.

"As soon as I surrender, I allow miracles to come into my life. I went through a hard, low time at the beginning of last year. It was the first time I felt so out of control, so down and depressed, so lacking in energy. There was nothing there for me. I wasn't even there for me.

"My knowledge then consisted of just struggling with it all, trying to get out of the trap of my feelings. Yet the day I affirmed that I would no longer fight with my feelings, but let them play their course, that was the day I allowed what I was going through, all of it, to teach me. In no time at all, I was feeling much better.

"We don't allow the natural rhythms of life to take their course. We think we should always be up and smiling and in control. Yet there is a natural expansion and a natural contraction in the universe. Birth rhythms are all about expansion and contraction. Expanding the birth canal, the contractions bearing down. We don't have one without the other. Both pave the way for new life. We need both expansion and contraction, even in the patient waiting process of the nine-month pregnancy cycle. The body expands outward, while at the same time the uterus contracts inward, softening the cervix.

"That's what life is all about, those natural expansions and contractions. But in our society, the contraction part of the process is seen as bad and wrong, and you struggle to get out of the contraction process and just get on with the expanding process. And we do this in every area of our lives. And often we feel like a failure, feel like we have fallen off our path in some way. That's crazy!

"Here we have this interview, and I feel so expansive, talking with you. But that's not the whole of life, that's not the whole of the miracle. That's only a part of it."

I ventured my own sense of the expansion and contraction ideas we had been exploring. "When I look behind whatever is going on in my own life — whether it be dealing with money issues, relationships, creativity, health, whatever — I can often see that I'm just in a different part of the process. And then

I choose — more and more, lately — to just be quiet and let myself flow into the learning rhythm again. To me, the very act of breath is the perfect expression of expansion and contraction. Breathing in is not better than or worse than breathing out. It's life! It's all life."

We nodded our heads in agreement.

Recently a phrase came to me in deep meditation that expresses the work that I am doing. I had been pouring energy out in both spontaneous and focused ways, through the joy and the discipline of writing this book and the joy and discipline of my personal responsibilities. I kept on going deep within, laboring, if you will, to find the energy needed to shape the stories and the ideas behind the stories so that the miracles in the stories would speak to the reader. And I got very tired, because I was pouring this energy out for so many months and making great changes in my personal life as well.

One morning I got up very early, before dawn, to meditate on what I could do to heal this deep tiredness within me. After some time of deep interior listening, these words came to me: "Strengthen the ground of your being." And tears rushed to my eyes, and a sob rose in my throat, because the inner message was so gentle and yet so powerful for me. I realized at that moment an intimate part of the process of tuning into miracles. Through all the stories and all the steps of observing and experiencing and, yes, trusting that the miracles would come, even through all of that learning time, I had not recognized the inflowing as well as the outflowing. It was time for me to receive. And so my deep, sweet, inner voice was telling me just what I needed, in the midst of all the miracles and in the midst of the birthing of the book, in the midst of the mystery of creation itself. I was being told, "Strengthen the ground of your being."

And that's the nurturing part of the mystery of creation. To expand and then go within. To give forth and then be still and receive. And to balance the process in the rhythm called life.

Death Is a Great Adventure

I warn you, if God gives you the grace to let go,
get ready for an unexpected transformation.

—MACRINA WIEDERKEN

When someone is dying, the circle is complete.

When someone is dying, there is a great and unique opportunity for miracles to take place for both the dying person and the family members. I am not talking about miraculous deathbed rescues, where the patient rises from the dead to walk again. Although there are certainly documented cases of remission and restoration, they are the rare exception.

Thich Nhat Hanh, a world-renowned Buddhist spiritual teacher, has this to say about the miracle of death: "We have to accept death; it makes life possible. The cells in our body are dying every day, but we never think to organize funerals for them. The death of one cell allows for the birth of another. Life and death are two aspects of the same reality."

Nowhere was that more evident to me than when I interviewed a remarkable eighty-three-year-old man named Joey. Joey was propped up in a hospital bed at his son's house, overlooking a garden. His son, who owned a home health-care nursing service, was with him, as well as a nurse, a caterer who had just delivered a beautiful lunch to tempt the old man to eat, and Joey's eighty-three-year-old girlfriend. Yes!

Joey had requested this interview because he wanted everyone out there to know that he had had a good life, an extraordinary life, a full life, and he had some wisdom to impart to everyone who would listen. Although he was dying of cancer and frequently had to stop to conserve his strength and breathe into an oxygen tube, I have never met a man who was more alive.

Before the interview I talked at length with Joey's son, David, who had set up the interview, and he told me about his remarkable father and where he was in his life process.

"My father was in show business. He started out with Milton Berle and Danny Thomas and all the rest of them, and though he achieved medium fame, he never quite made it to the big time. But that's something he's hung onto all these years, being an entertainer. Even two months ago he was still singing and dancing in old folks homes, just to entertain them. He was just loving his life! That's who he is, an entertainer. And he has so much invested in that part of his past, so much of his identity, that when I was talking about you coming to do this interview, he was asking me, 'Well, does she know that I'm an entertainer?'

"And I said, 'Now you need to know that she's coming here to talk to you about death, because you're so open about it. The thing that I would love for you to understand, that's so important, is that who you *were* was wonderful — you had great gifts of entertainment — but she doesn't know a thing about you, and she's coming because of who you are *today*. And who you are *today* is just as special and just as important as what you used to do and who you used to be.'

"I wanted him to realize that right now the gift he can give people in talking openly about death will be as powerful as any gift he ever gave in the thirties or forties. So I told him how I felt about his great gifts *now*.

"And he had to think about that for a moment or two, and then he grinned and said, 'Got it!' ""

"What else did he say?" I wanted to know.

"Let me give you some background. My father had a dream. Just a couple of months ago he was walking two miles a day, he would do shows, he loved to go to Vegas with his friends and have a good time, he was a man in love with life. But then he called me up in December and he said, 'I have to see you right away, Son.' And I said, 'What's wrong?' And he said, 'Well, let me just come down to L.A. and I'll tell you.' And I said, 'Sure, but I'm worried. What's wrong?' And he said, 'Well, I dreamed last night that I was about to die. I saw it all, and it was all real clear, and I feel like it's really true. I don't want this to be a tragedy. I feel it's my time, and I just want to come down and see you — and let's play.'

"So I agreed, and he flew here, and after about four days here we went to Vegas and spent five days there together and just had a great time together. And we talked about it all, the dream, his conviction that it was his time to die. I thought, 'Well, who knows if it's real or not, but you never know.' And it's just amazing that it turns out it looks like it *is* true. He is going to die.

"And later, after a heart attack, when he was in the hospital, that's when they found the cancer. One night we were talking in the intensive care unit, and we were laughing some and crying some. Then he went to sleep, and the doctor came in and told me the news. My father was sleeping, and I was crying, and he woke up and asked me, 'What's going on? Why are you crying?' And I pulled myself together somewhat, and I told him the truth about what the doctors and nurses had said. 'Well, your heart's not doing well tonight. And they don't think you're going to make it through the night.'

"He just laid there and looked at me for a minute or two, and then he said, 'Well, I don't know what to say. I've had a good life, and I've had eighty-three years, and you know you talk all the time about people with AIDS, the ones you work with in your service. They're dying at twenty-five. I have nothing to complain about.'

"Isn't that a remarkable statement from a dying man? 'I have nothing to complain about.'"

"Yes, it is," I said softly, thinking of the journey through my son's death that I had shared with him, his own courage, his own luminosity. David and I stared at each other with tears in our eyes as the words "I have nothing to complain about" echoed in the room.

David continued to tell me about that night. "And then we talked a little bit more and he said, 'Well, son, I know that this is going to be hard on you, but time heals.' Then he said, 'In a lot of ways in the past few years my life has been boring. I wake up every morning with the mind of a forty-year-old, and then I'm reminded that I'm an eighty-three-year-old man. I can't do the things I want to do. I can't be the person that I want to be anymore. It just feels right that it's time to move on.' Then we were both quiet for awhile. And finally he said to me, 'In a lot of ways I'm real excited about it.'

"So we started laughing and crying and reminiscing together and even speculating a little on what it would be like on the other side. We started exploring. We talked about death and the hereafter. We said to each other, 'Well, what do you think it's going to be like? Do you think that all of a sudden you'll be there on the other side and there will be Mom greeting you, and your parents and your brother? Or do you think that all of a sudden you'll just be this spirit or this light, and there will be another spirit or another light next to you, and you'll realize that this is the same feeling that you got from my mother, and you'll realize that it's her? Or you'll suddenly be surrounded by a warmth, and you'll realize that you haven't felt that particular warmth since your parents were here, on this side? And now they are there, with you, on the other side? What's it going to be like?'

"And then we talked about reincarnation too. 'What if you're going to wake up in this brand-new body raring to go? How exciting that will be!' And then he could start over. And we talked about all the old sayings, you know, like 'Youth is wasted on the young,' and what if he had a brand-new body but he had this great old wisdom, and 'If I knew then what I know now,' all those things. And we thought, 'What if you get to take all your experiences with you? What if you do get to wake up in a brand-new body with all this experience and get to be young again with all that you know? How incredible that will be!' We even wondered, 'Do you think there will be cities where you are going? How familiar or unfamiliar will it be?' We wondered and played with the possibilities all night long."

"How extraordinary!" I remarked.

"Right. And then, once we had gone through the painful part of it, well, the possibilities were endless. And it became more of a celebration of what was happening to him than a deathwatch. When I thought of him going to this other place, maybe taking all his experiences or maybe having a whole new body, I thought, 'It's really the miracle of death.' You know, you hear so much about the miracle of birth that no one thinks what a miracle death must be."

"I agree. Once I interviewed a woman who is a midwife to the dying, and she talked about that same process. And then I interviewed a woman who is a midwife to the birthing process, and they both agreed that the process is very similar. That there is indeed a miracle of death, just like there is a miracle of birth."

When I walked into Joey's presence, he grinned at me and waved from his hospital bed. And I smiled back at him. I knew then that for however long he was here on this earth I had found a dear friend. The room was full of joy, a luminous energy that I had experienced only once before, when my own dear son was dying. This energy of aliveness and joy permeated the conversation that followed.

Here is the gist of what he said to me.

"Look, I can only tell you in two words: I'm ready. I've been everywhere. I've seen everything. I've had money. I've had none. I've lived a life. What a life! All I want to do is just go onward and see what it's going to be like over there."

"Sounds to me like you're an adventurer."

"I certainly am. And look, I don't fear death. Are you kidding? If God took me off the earth this minute, he'd be doing me a favor. I know, I've read too much. I've seen too much. I know, and no one's going to kid me. There is life after death."

"Joey, I couldn't agree with you more."

"And here's what I'm going to tell you. There's got to be life after death. There's got to be! When you die, you go to a better place. You go to be with the ones you love. When we used to go to pray at a funeral, I would stand there and I would know, that the body was there, but the person had gone on. There was no one home! And all that was around that person, the air around that person, well, it was love. It's just love. That air is love. I saw my friend in the coffin, and I said, 'He's sleeping, but he's still blessed.' It was a blessing."

"Do you have an idea of what death will be for you?" I asked him. "What do you think it's going to be like?"

"Well, how could life here on earth be any different from the hereafter? Except that the hereafter won't have pain. I go by one thing. What God does. So I want to talk about my life and my death, but no one is going to cheat me out of my death. I'm ready when God is."

"Are you ready then to rush into the experience?"

"Are you kidding? I wish it would happen right now. I'd like to close my eyes and and that would be it. Because I want to tell you, I've lived a fabulous life. There's nothing I've missed in all this world, and all I can say is that I'm not like the average person who, the minute he gets real sick or is old and thinks he's going to die, calls in the priest, calls in the rabbi, is moaning and groaning and carrying on. The average person fears death. Not me. Because it's going to be so beautiful, more beautiful than you've ever known, on the other side. It's going to be wonderful. I think it's the most wonderful thing in the world. I can't wait."

"Do you think that that is the most important thing you can tell people about this experience, Joey? Because you're going to live forever in this book. I'm going to put down everything you say, so that other sons and daughters and people like me can really see how it can be. So I want to know what other words of wisdom you have for those of us who are facing death and for those of us who have loved ones who are facing death."

"Well, I have just one more thing to say to you, young lady. And it's important."

"I'm listening."

"You tell them all out there what I said. I have looked death in the face and I say, 'Wow! Death is a great adventure. I can hardly wait.' "

Joey died peacefully five days later.

The Dying Winner

It is not the end of the physical body that should worry us.
Rather, our concern must be to live while we're alive — to release our inner
selves from the spiritual death that comes from living behind a facade
designed to conform to external definitions of who and what we are.

—*Elisabeth Kübler-Ross*

All of us die. It is how we die that makes a difference. Even during our last, intense journey, we have the opportunity to give and receive courage and love. Both of these qualities are attributes of miracles. We have the opportunity to open to our deepest truths, and, eschewing the trivial, mundane concerns of everyday life, we have an opportunity to live our last moments in communion with others.

This is what happened to a friend of mine mentioned earlier, whose professional work takes him into hospital cancer wards to be with both families and patients on the last journey. Here is what he told me.

"Our culture teaches us that death is the ultimate failure. Both doctor and patient fight desperately to save the body at all costs. The family becomes a part of the process of fighting to the last breath. And yet this fight is the most unrealistic one we will ever encounter.

"I tried to tell this to one man — a man who was dying in my arms, surrounded by his family, a man who had fought so hard against cancer and was now at the point where he had to surrender and let go of his body. I told him that he was a winner.

"I told him," and here tears came into my friend's eyes, "I told him *that he had changed the world.* By his very presence, by his life here on this earth, by his love and concern for others, he had changed the world.

"He looked around at his family, smiled tremulously, tried to hold out his arms to them. His wife was on one side, I was on the other, holding him. His children and grandchildren were gathered around the bed. He looked at each of them, and said softly, 'I love you.' And then he died peacefully in my arms.

"And then I realized that he had changed *my* life as well. He had forced me to move from a detached state of caregiving into an overwhelming expression of God's love at work in my life.

"The words I told him echoed within me. 'You have changed the world.' From that moment onward, I began to see that everyone I came in contact with in that hospital setting, in my private practice, and in the personal areas of my life, had changed the world as well. By their very presence they had changed the lives of those around them. By their love and dignity they had changed the world. And I thought what a wonderful epitaph for each of us, to know without a shadow of a doubt that we had made a difference in our lives and in the lives of those we loved, that the world was a better place for our having been there, that our loved ones, even while grieving, were enriched by our presence on the planet. And that was a real bona fide, never-to-be-forgotten miracle for me."

"Would it have been a miracle if the man had lived?" I asked my friend, who on his rounds had occasion to witness life at its most devastating.

"No," he said. "It would have been a tragedy. His body was not capable of sustaining life. He would have been in agonizing, ever-increasing pain. The miracle was in his love for his family and his recognition that his life meant something, that he had fought the good fight, and now he could rest in the arms of the angels. The miracle was in his knowing not only that he was loved and cherished and cared for in the last moments of his life, but that he could extend love outward to others at the very moment of his death. I hope that I will have the opportunity to die like that man died, giving and receiving love, knowing that his life mattered. His miracle lives on in those of us who were there with him as he passed peacefully onward into another dimension.

"Working in the cancer ward allows me to see miracles every day, in the most intense instances of human interaction and human courage. I am blessed by having known this man, this man who changed the world by his presence. And when it is my time to go, I hope with all my heart that I can both give and receive love in the last moments of my life."

I asked him if he had ever seen angels in the hospital or at the bedside of those who were about to go onward.

"Oh absolutely," he replied. "Angels often walk the halls of the acute-care ward and hover around the bedsides of dying patients. You can sense and feel their presence, even when you can't see them. There seems to be an outpouring of love from on high when the angels come. I believe that they are the helpers of infinite care who escort us from life on earth to life hereafter. Sometimes I think that the angels are like midwives. They help people into a new birth, just as we are helped into birth on this plane by loving hands. Even in the midst of my own private challenges, I feel an enormous sense of peacefulness that permeates my life. I know it's because the angels are nearby.

"And here is the best part," he continued. "Maybe it was a result of that particular man's death, the one we talked about, but I have come to a realization: We are all angels. Or at least we can be. We are all angels to each other. I think we help the angels to do their jobs here. And then they help us at the end of life, when we need their nurturing presence most."

I contemplated his words. When we are open to miracles in the midst of a loved one's last and ultimate journey, when we are open to miracles in the midst of pain and loss and grief, when we are open to miracles no matter what happens, then we too, can begin to see and sense and feel and hear angels. When we are open to miracles, we can all be angels to one another. And that will indeed change the world.

Trusting in Miracles

Be patient toward all that is unresolved in your heart.
Try to love the questions themselves....
Do not seek the answers which cannot be given,
Because you would not be able to live them.
And the point is, to live everything.
Live the questions now.
Perhaps you will then,
Gradually, without noticing it,
Live along some distant day
Into the answers.

—Rainer Maria Rilke

What did I learn from interviewing ordinary people, touched by miracles, all over the country? I have as many questions as I have answers. For it is grappling with the questions of life that teaches us what we really believe. About God, about angels, about a higher force for good. About everything that constitutes a miracle.

As I grow older, and hopefully wiser, I have come to believe that there is a simple explanation for miracles. While we wait to win the lottery or to be saved from an automobile crash, while we wait for the dying to arise and walk and the sick to be healed, while we wait for the pounds to fall off miraculously and the beloved to return, while we wait and watch and wonder, while we pray in whatever ways we have been taught, miracles come stealing into our hearts and our souls. Sometimes they are not the kind of miracles we have prayed for. Sometimes they do not fit our limited ideas of what we think we really need. But as we recognize our miracles, however hard-won, we open to renewal.

I believe that a variety of circumstances opens us to miracles. I believe in holy relationships and satisfying work and the kindness of both strangers and friends. And I believe that prayer, meditation, contemplation, and the wise blessings within both our waking and our sleeping dreams are also avenues to miracles.

We all have different styles of prayer. But whether we entreat someone above to hear our prayer or sit quietly in the silence, whether we ask for and receive the answers in our dreams or in our daily walks, whether we pray through our loving actions to others on our rounds at work or go up on a mountaintop and open to receive the divine spirit, each of us is constantly and continually learning the way of miracles.

Through our life lessons, through our life challenges, through our quiet moments, through our interactions with others, through our selflessness, and through our self-reflection, we are learning miracles.

In an earlier book, *Soulwork*, I wrote about three areas of life that must be addressed as we move from an unconscious reaction to life to a conscious awareness of our individual, integral part in the universe.

We must, if we so choose, clear our minds of learned patterns of behavior and rote thought that keep us from recognizing miracles all around us. Then we must, if we so choose, open our hearts so that our connections to others are made with a full, rich giving and receiving, a full flowing of ourselves, one to another. Then we must, without a doubt, replenish our spiritual lives, filling our souls with both grace and goodness. This process takes a lifetime, but it is richly rewarded.

At the very beginning of this book, when I set out with paper and pen and tape recorder to interview and share with friends and strangers their stories of miracles, I felt a sense of wonder and expectancy, not knowing what I would find. I felt like one of those spiritual pilgrims of old, who search all their lives for the truth within the mystery of life itself, who search all their lives for the grace of God. And like the people I met along the way, whose stories touched my heart as I hope and pray they will touch yours, I moved from observing to experiencing to finally and irrevocably trusting in miracles.

We are all spiritual pilgrims.

In opening to miracles, we open to the best within us. We open to life! We live the questions, and some distant day we will, as Rainer Maria Rilke says, live into the answers. Then everything that we do and everything that we are and everything that we aspire to be is an expression of love, and thus an expression of a miracle in the making. Then we are both blessing and miracle. And our lives are changed forever.

HOW TO MAKE A MIRACLE

Decide what you want. Be specific. Sit down and be still. Ask for what you want.
Determine, if you can, that anything you ask, be for good, and only for good,
not for harm, not for manipulation. Only for good.

❧

Ask for guidance. Ask God, Jesus Christ, your guardian angel, your
Higher Power, your highest self, the light. Don't ask how. Don't ask why.
Ask for what you want. Listen. Don't beg. Don't plead. Listen.

❧

Ask what, if any, are the character defects, obstacles, and blocks that stand in
your way. Ask to be shown how to remove them or go around them.

❧

Be willing to change. Be willing to clear up your clutter, your inertia,
your fears, your guilt, your grief, your resentments. Ask for help.
Ask for clarity. Ask for clear perception. Continue.

❧

Pledge your hands, your head, and your heart to this endeavor.
Mind alone will not do it. Emotion alone will not do it.
Physical action alone will not do it.

❧

Be willing to serve. Be willing to do your part. Be willing to let your talents
flourish and bear fruit. Be willing to reap what you sow. Be willing to give to
others. Be willing to give to the world. Be willing to give to yourself.

Be willing to change. Ask again and again for the highest good of all concerned, whatever your prayer may be. Ask to be shown the way. Ask for this or something better.

Forgive. Forgive others. Forgive yourself. Forgive the past. Forgive God.

Ask that light fill the vessel of your being.
Ask that your prayer be answered in wisdom and love.

Ask what you can do specifically, concretely, now, to open to a miracle. What can you delete, add, clear up, clear out, shift, release, rethink? What can you give? What can you receive? What is the truth of this situation? Wait. Listen. Receive the answers.

Get up. Act on the wisdom you have received. Be alert. Watch for opportunities, signs, portents. Show up. Stand up and be counted. Flow into the opportunities. Move. Throw yourself forward into sweet service.

Then rest. Let it happen. Let it come.

When what you wished for, hoped for, prayed for shows up in front of you, refrain from surprise. Recognize it. Take it. Receive. Accept. Give thanks. Do the work. Continue.

LIST OF CONTRIBUTORS

Many of the people I interviewed for this book prefer to remain anonymous. In some cases, stories from individuals whose names I didn't know or who had already made their transition touched my heart, even as their families and caregivers shared their stories with me. Stories of great difficulty and great change and transformation are continuing miracles. As are my own personal miracle stories, which you may catch a glimpse of throughout this book. So this list of contributors is incomplete, although their stories continue to bless and inspire all of us. To all contributors, many, many thanks! May miracles continue to come your way!

Damiella Datskovskaya Ackerman
Marc Allen
Bob Anderson
Catherine Anderson
Phil Catalfo
Helen Cook
Connie Courtney
Karel Eastman
Bonnie Hampton
Sandy Denke Jones

Emily LeVier
Raymond LeVier
Alice McGinnis
Richard Nesta
Rita Robinson
Debby Roth
Joey Shea
Irma Torres
Herman Weiner

ABOUT THE AUTHOR

BettyClare Moffatt, M.A., is a prominent writer
and public speaker in the fields of AIDS, death and dying,
grief recovery, and women's spirituality. She is the author of
Soulwork: Clearing the Mind, Opening the Heart, Replenishing the Spirit;
When Someone You Love Has AIDS: A Book of Hope for Family and Friends;
Gifts for the Living: Conversations with Caregivers on Death and Dying;
and several other books. She divides her time between
Texas, New Mexico, and California.

Interior by Poulson/Gluck Design.
Cover by Sharon Smith Design.

The text is Berkeley Book.
Titles and quotes are Schneidler Italic.

Printed by Data Reproductions Corporation,
Rochester Hills, Michigan.

Wildcat Canyon Press and New World Library
are dedicated to publishing books and audio cassettes
that help improve the quality of our lives. For a catalog
of our fine books and cassettes, contact:

New World Library
Wildcat Canyon Press
58 Paul Drive
San Rafael, CA 94903

Phone: (415) 472-2100
Fax: (415) 472-6131

Or call toll free: (800) 227-3900